The Rollright Ritual

William Gordon Gray

This edition published in Great Britain in 2011 by Skylight Press,
210 Brooklyn Road, Cheltenham, Glos GL51 8EA

First published in 1975 by Helios Book Service, Toddington, Cheltenham, Glos.

Designed and typeset by Rebsie Fairholm
Cover and title page photographs by Matt Baldwin-Ives
Interior photographs (from the original edition) by Lee James
Illustration by Linda Wheeler

With thanks to Helios Book Service for access to their archive materials.

Printed and bound in Great Britain by Lightning Source, Milton Keynes

www.skylightpress.co.uk

ISBN 978-1-908011-17-6

CONTENTS

Publisher's note: This edition of *The Rollright Ritual* is the complete and unabridged original text, as published in 1975. Any references to contemporary life which may now be outdated have been retained as written; we have also retained W. G. Gray's style of capitalising certain words for emphasis. In addition to all the original photographs, we have included two images of the Rollright stones which were submitted by W. G. Gray for the original publication but not used.

&FOREWORD

The famous Stone Circle of the "Rollrights" in Oxfordshire near a village of that name is well known to folklorists. The tale of the old witch who turned a King and his entire entourage into three sets of Stones, a single one for the King, several together for his nobles, and a big circle for all his men is more than worn out with repetition. So are most of the other stories about them. New and modern mythologies stemming from science-fictional roots are attaching more meanings still. Anything from flying saucer depots to advanced astronomical calculators are guessed at and written up. This account is along entirely different lines altogether.

It is the outcome of many years' personal contact with the Stones themselves on "Inner" levels of investigation. Slowly and steadily a story told itself piece by piece which made the soundest possible spiritual sense, and opened up entirely new areas of awareness through the oldest doors available to enquiring consciousness. The story concerns our deepest fundamentals as humans on this Earth, and how the Stones came to stand for our purpose in Life on this planet. Moreover, it shows unmistakably that far from being a mere "ancient monument," the Stones outline a permanent Pattern leading to our ultimate perfection as people.

In a normal and natural way, the Stones spoke through their own symbology of what they stood for in the past, and how this infallibly indicates the future we could expect if we are willing to follow the Pattern they laid out so long ago. Since the enquirer in this case was a working magical ritualist, the Stones revealed their ancient ritual structure translated into timeless terms of truth with the most startling spiritual significance and an intense impact of authenticity. It was an experience altogether "out of this world" to undergo. No words can possibly express the sense of "Inner reality and sincerity" felt during the Inner encounters with what can only be called the "Spirit of the Stones". This story comes straight from the heart and soul of an appreciative and everlastingly grateful human hearer who listened to the Stones themselves telling it in their own strange silent speech. What they had to say makes a message our modern world might do well to heed. Let all judge for themselves its value.

It is only fair to say that the fundamentals of what follows were found before the Stones were fenced off against vandalism by their recent and hideous enclosure. There is no doubt a need was felt to protect them against senseless and wanton depredations including fierce fires built against some of the Stones, and actual removal of smaller rocks in the circle. What is regrettable is the lack of taste and totally inartistic palisades put up which do virtually nothing to deter wilful destructors and entirely ruin all traces of romance previously perceptible around the place. Perhaps time will soften such stringency. The Stones have outlived far worse ill-treatment. In any case their message is immortal and applicable anywhere else in existence. That can never be destroyed now that something of it has been preserved for posterity.

The outsides of the Stones may be met with by anybody, but it is the Insides of them which tell the true story of what they mean for Mankind. Here is what was heard by a modern member of what might perhaps be called their "secret Circle". Let others go and listen for themselves who will. They need not go so far as the Stones. The story will equally unfold in a backyard or within a mind laid out as this perceived Pattern explains in detail. Anybody can make a Rollright Circle anywhere they will, if indeed they are so spiritually inclined. Here are all the hows, whys and wherefores as received by a modern occult observer of the same Western Tradition from whence the Inner structure of the Stones originally sprang so long ago.

CHAPTER ONE
ℭIRCLING ᵴTONES

Making circles from stones is probably among the most primitive and instinctive practices known to Man. Nowadays we impute all kinds of involved motivations for this, ranging from the most elaborate astronomical calculations to landing sites for "flying saucers". The fundamental basics of circle-building are far simpler than either supposition. It stems from a sense of Self-assertion within a protective perimeter of perception which determines the establishment of an Identity as distinct from all else in existence. Even now, we draw rings round figures or phrases so as to "single them out" for attention by observers. Before Man ever put pencil to paper, he was outlining himself with pebbles in order to focus the attention upon himself of that Infinite Awareness which he felt so strongly and certainly everywhere around him.

Man is firstly aware of his own being as a contrasting consciousness to all else in his experience of existence. A "Me and Thee" sort of outlook on Life. Somewhere between these two extremities of awareness there logically has to be a dividing principle distinguishing one from the other. In the case of a human body for instance, its skin is the last line of demarcation between the living being inside it, and all other living beings outside it. Physically, we can touch our skins and say more or less: "This is where I stop and everybody else begins their relationship with me." What can we do spiritually to give us an equivalent sense of "Me and Thee-ness"? Only trace a hypothetical Circle round ourselves and consider this a Symbol of whatever distinguishes us from the rest of Creation and all other consciousness than ours circulating through the whole of Cosmos. A genuine Magical Circle in the true meaning of the term. Since early Man on Earth had only sticks and stones to make patterns of, these were what he made his circles with. Sticks, being what they are, perished long ago, but the Stones are with us still, so they will have to answer the questions we are asking from our present point of Time-Space-Events connecting us with them through our Cosmic continuum.

Early Man formed very close relationships with ordinary stones which we might find a little difficult to appreciate in our times. Stones were so deeply involved with the living-patterns of those far-off days that no form of culture or civilisation would have been possible without them. They were a universal material obtainable at all seasons in all places. Stones and reliability became linked together in evolving human consciousness. Both for defensive and offensive purposes, stones enabled Mankind to establish a survival procedure on the surface of this earth. With a good sharp stone in each hand, humans felt their chances of living among so many hostile or dangerous fellow-creatures had decidedly improved. There was also nothing like a nice solid chunk of rock between an otherwise defenceless human, and something else with a huge hungry mouth full of long teeth needing exercise. Today maybe, we might compare this with the sense of relative security provided by several hundred feet of rock, steel, and concrete between humans and a threatened atomic attack. Circumstances alter, but principles prevail.

Early adventurers into the unknown wild world away from their birthplace soon learned how to sojourn or sleep surrounded by handy heaps of stone missiles for the sake of their safety. No matter from which quarter danger threatened, a defensive fusillade of stones could be kept up while ammunition lasted, and quite large or unlikely creatures would be driven off or discouraged by such means. Even a single hunter gathered as many stones around himself as possible before settling for the night. In point of fact, a pebbly place was about the safest spot to be on dark dangerous nights, because nothing large enough to be a menace could approach remotely without enough crunching noises to betray its presence for miles. One had to learn these facts at an early age in those days, or one was never likely to live until the advanced age of twenty-five, or even an incredibly ancient thirty Solar seasons. When stones and survival went together, the former had high priority with those seeking the latter.

As with all our survival-patterns, what worked on Earth in this world might be expected to extend into those Inner dimensions of existence which Man instinctively realised held all the hopes for his future in any condition of conscious Identity. If circles of stones made life easier here, then they should do so in the "Elsewhere". A very logical assumption for primitive people relating themselves between physical and metaphysical consciousness. From this point on, it was only a question of evolution as to how the stone circles developed along increasingly sophisticated lines involving both angles of awareness.

At one time among some of the aboriginals, when a woman was about to give birth she was taken some way into the bush by her female companions, who cleared a small circle of soft sand over which she squatted while they gave what help they might think of. Around the edge of the sand-circle small stones were arranged as a protective perimeter. These stones were left *in situ* and later on, if the child lived and grew old enough, it was shown its birthplace circle and told that this was its very own Earth-spot where it "landed" from spirit-space. If ever it were in difficulties or in need of "spirit communion", this was its proper place to go and ask for Inner aid. A very lovely idea altogether, and most probably the commencement of the "pilgrimage instinct" inherent in humanity, amounting to a belief that if only the right place and occasion can be found, troubles, illnesses, and other evils may be averted and negated from those placing themselves under the protection of whatever Power presides there.

Whether a single sorrowful human crept quietly away to his secret stone circle, or a whole troubled tribe got together in their common encirclements, the basic idea of coming into close contact with Primal Parenthood whether personalised as Sky-Father and Earth-Mother, or in any other way, for the sake of satisfying some deep spiritual life-need, continued to motivate successive generations of Circle gatherers. That they must have found some form of satisfaction is evident from the remains of so many such Circles, and the undoubted existence of thousands more long since broken up in the course of our civilisations. Probably our progenitors had far more genuine Inner returns and benefits from their primitive arrangements than we are able to obtain from our synthetic and unstable substitutes today. At least they felt confident that they were taking themselves and their affairs into circles where Gods and fellow humans really cared about them personally, and were truly concerned with their problems and issues on individual life-levels. Can we do as much today?

Any thinking person of our times realises only too well how human individualism is threatened on a world-wide scale with "economic elimination." The whos, hows, and whys, of this process are matters for consideration elsewhere. It is sufficient that for present purposes we should admit awareness of this spiritual danger, and determine to seek some sensible means of counteraction. Since the old Stone Circles were constructed for and dedicated to the solution of personal survival-problems both from material and spiritual life-level, it seems a good idea to approach them for any practical suggestions in applying their principles to the preservation of our own identities through these perilous ages. They may well have more to tell us now than they had so long ago. So much of our history and experience has begun in, developed around, and flowed through them, that they must have absorbed some of our characteristic energies with the passing of time, much as meaning is now impressed on magnetic tape. If a suitable recall system is available, all this material may be "played back" in terms of comprehensible consciousness.

The principles of this have been known in broad outline for a long while. Basically, the activities of our consciousness modify the energy-fields around us, and in some way not yet understood, residuals of these may remain connected with the structures of actual physical substances either environmentally or otherwise exposed to the original influence. It is analogous to impressing processes of consciousness into brain cells, or the energies of sound and light into appropriate recording materials. Some materials "take" these impressions better and more durably than others, stone being evidently fairly high in this category. Again, certain classes of stone seem to be definitely related with specific types or frequencies of consciousness. Hence all the instinctive Magic with talismans and "charms", most of which had gem-stones incorporated in them somewhere. There is a great amount of most valuable knowledge waiting to be rediscovered along these lines by new awareness applied to an ancient art.

What all this came to in simple terms was that in some mysterious manner stones acted as storage agencies of human and possibly non-human energies of consciousness. Say, for example, someone in early times picks up a stone never touched by human hands before, and while holding it has some very powerful emotional experience involving considerable expenditure of Inner energies. We will suppose a sudden feeling of hatred for a fellow tribesman and inclinations to murder him with the stone being held. For some reason a negative decision is reached and the stone dropped. Now it has become a rather special stone, because its invisible component is highly charged with energies attuned to antipathy toward some particular person. Once more let us suppose a little while later some relatively sensitive being picks up the same stone and regards it receptively from little other motive than curiosity. Everything depends on what sort of individuals they are as to how they will react to the influences "picked up" from the stone. Some might feel an unaccountable sensation of hostility, others an unexplained and unconnected desire to kill or injure some unknown person. Others again, merely a fear for their own lives. There are very many possible reactions. It is just conceivable that an enemy of the first intended victim might pick up the stone, and while playing around with it receive sufficient extra energy to decide him definitely on a murder mission. All sorts of potentials exist where charges of consciousness are concerned.

Undoubtedly in earlier times some of the brighter observers came to the conclusion that stones which had seemed to speak with "God-voices", could also contain at least the gist of human intentions when these were deliberately applied with effort over prolonged periods. This discovery meant that if they set up special stones for particular purposes, these ought to establish contact with whatever "God-Concept" as we should say now, dealt with that special subject or intention. For instance, if a natural or roughly shaped chunk of stone were set up and dedicated to the Mother-Deity alone, and none allowed to touch, approach, or even think about the artifact except in ways or with intentions appropriate to this Concept, then the total force of its accumulated Inner energy would be focused to this end entirely. This meant much more magnified results if practised by a whole tribe, than if by only one person.

The implications and possibilities behind this very elementary practice were, and still are, quite astounding. It means that a primitive two-way communicator of consciousness can be established between very different dimensions of Life. A simple stone held the secret in those days, just as quartz crystals hold the secrets of our telecommunications today. The methods, of course, are entirely at variance, though perhaps arising from common principles. Nowadays we have complicated equipment to do the job for us. Then, they just kept directing their contact and consciousness into a stone, and relied purely on their Inner sensitivities to make intelligible meanings out of what returned to them therefrom. This may sound crude to our ideas, but it worked for early inhabitants of Earth with minds uncluttered and unspoiled by the corroding complexities of our modern civilisations.

So, in quite a reasonable way, began human customs of consciousness which later degenerated (like so many others) into confusional idolatry. To some extent, the huge stylised stones sculpted into figures representing the aims and ideals of maybe an entire nation were always practical propositions for focusing Inner energies, but the sheer inadequacy or incompatibility of human awareness applied to them, usually made them even worse than futile. With enough ill-intentions, destructive inclinations, and other evilly-motivated energies concentrated in them, these enormous stone condensers of consciousness could become a positive menace to their human congregations. All they did when charged with such injurious influences was to affect people in a bad, rather than good way.

Initiated individuals realised this to various degrees, but were scarcely able to prevent practice which had by this time become the "pop-culture" of its period. Therefore, instead of the old open Circles where all comers were once welcome, the Closed Circles of the Mysteries only admitting chosen and dedicated souls sprang up. Even these could not be entirely successful, despite all precautions against human fallibilities, but at least they operated along far finer lines than Inner areas contaminated with the confused and conflicting consciousness of the "mindless masses" all struggling for stupid, greedy, or other un-spiritual ends.

Possibly one of the most sophisticated methods of making up protected perimeters of Inner power in old times was the famous Temple of the Israelites, developed from much older techniques. There were no God-Images because everyone was supposed to acknowledge Divinity as the Life-Spirit recognisable in and as Life itself. No necessity for stone Figures existed because the whole Temple was constructed of that very material, and therefore condensed the consciousness of the congregation quite adequately. Those people were roughly graded into categories, only the most suitable being allowed closest to the centre. The physical nucleus round which the whole metaphorical Circle revolved was a stone chamber holding nothing but a few very simple Symbols. Only one human being, the High Priest, ever entered this "Holy of Holies" on one brief occasion each year when, in the name of all his people, he uttered no more than the Name of their Deity, whose Presence was presumed to be particularly pronounced in that sacred place.

There are almost innumerable instances of stones being employed as localisers and condensers of consciousness extending between human and other states of awareness. The Urim and Thummim (Lights and Truths) of the High Priest's breastplate are examples. So is the legendary stone pillow of Jacob, who dreamed of angels thereon. Gazing-stones of all descriptions, including our modern crystals, have been in use right down the ages. Perhaps less obviously put to such purposes are tombstones of every type from the mightiest Pyramid to the humblest headstone. Humans still instinctively feel a sense of personal contact between the living and the dead by means of a standing stone commemorating the departed. This is more than merely memory, or "substitute symbolism", being a deep and inherent idea that the actual stone provides some kind of agency capable of linking the consciousness of living people with that of whoever the stone stands for. Centuries ago, commemorative communion services were held periodically on tombstones, and the altar-tomb is still a familiar feature of our churchyards. The Christian type of altar itself is tomb-like from its associations with the catacombs, and signifies the presence of Divinity in Whom Mankind hopes for immortality.

This function of stone as a condenser and conveyor of consciousness is really the secret component of the old stone Circles. Each stone became "charged" for some special reason by a particular person, people, or purpose. It had its "Key-note", and all subsequent variations on that theme added over the course of time. Sensitive subjects could "pick up" and interpret these to quite an extent. Others were aware of them, but unable to sort them into any particular sense. Yet others again scarcely felt any definite impact from these influences, but realised well enough they existed, and took for granted they were meant to benefit those who assembled within the environs of their energy. As a whole, people gathered about their Stones because they were convinced they could put something of themselves into these standing Symbols, and get something out in return which was well worth their trouble and effort in travel and expenditure of energy.

A very noteworthy example of this in modern times is the Wailing Wall in Jerusalem and the reactions of Israeli soldiers who captured that quarter of the city during the Six Day War. It was almost incredible how these men experienced all sorts of strange spiritual sensations when they encountered the Wall and realised they had "won it back" on behalf of their people. Far from being religious fanatics, many of the men were self-confessed atheists, agnostics, and disbelievers in any kind of Divine dispensations. Their roots were racial, not religious. These iron-hard, toughened, and ruthlessly disciplined soldiers confessed afterwards with something like embarrassment how those sole remaining stones of the old Temple had affected them. They did not try and explain why they felt as they did about a few stones. Few of them found words adequate to express themselves. One said significantly, "I felt as if all my ancestors were standing there right behind me." All agreed that in some mysterious way they did not pretend to grasp, the achievement of the Wall was the highlight and consummation of the entire campaign. Many said they felt silly in speaking of stones in such a fashion when so many human lives had been lost around them—yet they still spoke of the stones which connected them with their long-dead compatriots. It genuinely puzzled and concerned some of them why they should experience such strange and unexpected emotions about such unspectacular stones. Few except the fervent believers had anticipated having any particular feeling about the Wall. In their case, emotive enthusiasm is easy to understand, but the somewhat shyly sincere confidences of the soldiers strike a very deep chord indeed from the comprehending heart.

On a much lighter but still relevant level, is the common practice of professional crystal-gazers who place their glass globe in the client's hands for a few minutes before beginning a reading. It might be supposed this is a purely psychological trick to put the clients' minds into a calm condition and persuade them to concentrate on whatever they were concerned with. So it is to a great extent, but in addition this contact results in fractional charges of energy from the client being transferred to the crystal itself, and if the scryer be sufficiently sensitive, he or she may be able to "pick up" and interpret these energies in terms of thought relating to the individual imparting them. Whatever this faculty is called, by fancy names such as psychometry, ESP, or anything else, no one yet knows exactly how it works. Although the energies involved do not seem to have physical characteristics, actual physical contact with the charged influenced object appears necessary for obtaining optimum effect. Perhaps closest personal proximity making a closed circuit of consciousness between subject, object, and sensitive might be a fair description of required conditions. Although all kinds of metals, minerals, and materials seem to be "readable", the most reliable so far discovered is still stone. Whether this is due to its atomic structure, its durability, or some yet unknown property, is most uncertain. That it can and does retain recorded patterns of something connected with human and other types of consciousness seems reasonably certain. It is the investigation and interpretation of these which presents us with a set of most intriguing problems.

Relevant factors indicate so far that all different species of physical materials tend to retain or record impressions from different levels of human or other types of conscious energy. If we consider this like a spectrum or scale with broad basic frequencies, rising to higher and finer modifications of force as it leaves the upper limitations of our reachable range, we shall have a reasonable theoretical background to work against. As we might expect, plain common stone seems to associate mainly with our most basic, primitive, and fundamental frequencies of awareness, and this is the impressional level we are most likely to encounter when dealing with stones. Not that these are to be despised, belittled, or undervalued in the slightest degree. All our finest and most cultured states of consciousness are but refinements and developments of these primal potencies, and we could not conceive anything at all without them. Nevertheless, it must always be borne in mind while attempting "stone reading", that our direct receptions from them will be mainly from these categories of consciousness, and any intellectual or more formal interpretations we overlay them with, are probably from our own store of imagery. This can and does give quite satisfactory results, providing we realise precisely what is happening, and do not demand unreasonable productions from the practice.

Since we have not yet devised any instrumentation which will pick up and present these inherent psycho-physical energies in any kind of audio-visual way, we shall have to rely on the old fashioned methods of interpretation. Ostensibly, this is no more than making physical contact with the subject via fingertips and forehead, and intentionally seeking conscious contact with whatever may be translatable from it into terms of our thinking. The actual technique involved, however, is a little more complicated and exact than might appear from outside appearances.

In the first place, we are trying to get something out of the stone and into our awareness of what it means in relation to our minds. The stone will not work this transition for us, we have to do it ourselves. It may be useful to think of tape-recorder principles here. The magnetic tape does not actually make any sounds at all. What it does is modify the electronic energy which is capable of causing the end effect of sound. So with our stones. All they will do is modify the currents of consciousness we are releasing from our self-source and receiving back through the stone in question. How well or otherwise we manage this, how we contrive to transfer the re-recorded results into our subconscious store of awareness, and whatever may develop from this, depends entirely upon our skill and ability in the art. Some souls are naturally facile at this, and others have to plod along patiently until they acquire some proficiency by sheer hard practice. It is really a perfectly normal process of learning anything about anything. We are simply putting an ordinary faculty to somewhat uncommon usage.

If, say, the stone we are investigating were a book with printed information on its pages which we intended to study, our procedure would be clear enough. Assuming an ability of reading, mental attention must be confined to the text, and at least the gist of this transferred to and held by our internal reference banks of consciousness. Once safely installed there in correct categories, we can work with these impressions as we will. The important thing is to build up our memory banks before we can start spending their conscious capital. It used to be said that we "absorb" knowledge, and so we do in the sense that we receive and retain energies translatable into thought-terms. During this "take-in" process, the force-flow of our awareness has to be switched over to "Receive". It is of course possible to set our consciousness selectively, so that we shall receive along specified frequencies only, like a radio, though this takes a lot of practice and arrangement of mental circuitry. As a rule, in the case of book-work, pre-selection and sequential presentation of subject matters have already been attended to by authors and editors. Thus, we have only to "take it in" successfully, and sort everything out for ourselves subsequently. With stones, we have to take in what we can reach and clarify what we get into conscious conclusions according to our capabilities. In its way, this may be just as informative as mental material obtained by printed pages, and it was the only method available to mankind before words were ever written.

In the case of a printed book, our attention is held with it via our sense of sight. We direct the circuit of our consciousness towards it in a visual manner and receive our information in return through the same channel. If we read the words aloud we synchronise our audio-receptors with the incoming currents of consciousness to enhance the whole effect by this extra intake. When dealing with stones, our physically involved sense is principally touch. Hearing may also be linked up by rhythmical tapping on the stone in order to engage attention therewith in a definite pattern of awareness. Nowadays, this may be done with an electromechanical vibrator, especially one having a variable frequency. Quite interesting results can be obtained with this accessory if the forehead is pressed against the stone while the vibrations are passed through the stone via bone conductivity into the head, which stimulates both aural and tactile senses together. Investigation along these lines seems likely to offer future leads. It is doubtful, however, if the actual physical vibrations have any great effect in directly imparting impressions from the stone into the area of consciousness which concerns us here. They chiefly focus attention to the stone. Those who are able to keep consciousness focused at will may find silence the best background for reception. The technique of stone reading consists largely of trying to find and follow consciously whatever intangible impressions the stone contains as if it were a book, but not in direct terms of words or pictures. Simply as pure reactive summations in ourselves to the energies we encounter. This is very important. Most instructions connected with psychometry or ESP more or less suggest that articles should be held against the forehead, or otherwise contacted, the mind made as blank as possible, and inner visualisations or audio-ideas allowed to rise as they will in the mental field of reception so formed. This may and often does produce quite impressive or vivid scenic effects, but it does not develop the fundamental faculty of working with will along the deep-down levels of awareness far beyond our audio-visual range of perception. To reach those depths of reality it is necessary to "speak the silent tongue", sometimes called the "Old Language", which communicates by means of auto-recognitions of self-states between separate sources of consciousness. This happens quite apart from visualisations or verbalisations, which arise from interpretative imagery superimposed symbolically upon these basic themes of thinking in order to relate them with our ordinary world of wakeful working.

Lovers communicate with each other in this oldest of languages. They need not speak a word or see anything at all. It is enough for them that they feel and know what passes between them. That tells them everything they need to realise whatever concerns them with Cosmic Life. They are living beyond either sounds or sights. Touch-consciousness alone puts them in contact with everything in Existence which relates them with the state of Reality they seek as an integrative identity together. Something akin to this condition of consciousness is needed for successful communication with the "inner intelligence" concentrated in stones or any other form of physical corpus. The Magic "key" opening these normally closed portals leading to an incredible "world behind the world", is really Love. Love opens the gates of life everywhere, and when it is properly applied in its right degree, it will even let us into the secrets hidden by the humblest of stones.

This issue must be very closely and carefully understood before any attempts at putting it in practice are made. Otherwise no useful outcome may be expected, and possibly more harm than good done. Though no exact definition of "Love" can ever describe this Life-power with any certainty, let everyone accept the term according to his or her individual beliefs, and grant that there are degrees and variations of Love extending in all directions of existence. We may love Divinity Itself in one way, our fellow humans in another, other creatures in other ways, and even our enemies in different ways again. The diversities of Love are as infinite as Life, and we only know a very few of these on Earth. Therefore, to say that we should approach even stones with loving intent in order to learn their secrets is not so inapposite as it might seem.

It is a question of objectives and means of attainment. Love is a polarised power alternating between need and fulfilment. Be the need what it may, its fulfilment is whatever balances it back into beatific equilibrium. To love, we must need, though needs must not be confused with wants, nor does it follow that all needs arise from love alone unless we take the term in its absolute sense, since Love and Life are of a single Origin. The object of any love-effort should be the peaceful power-poise following its fulfilment. To this end ought its energies to be directed. The means by which it achieves such an end are not love-objectives, but facilities or channels by which ends are reached. We may love through them, with them, or however we care to employ their agencies, but they will always be accessories rather than aims of love. As such we may respect, admire, or even venerate them, but to treat them as love-objectives would only short-circuit our energies into ineffectuality, and lose contact with the Inner realities they represent. So our stones, or any form they may suggest, are usable accessories and material means for the energies we direct through them with a loving intention of reaching our Inner objective, which is the fulfilment of our need for contact with the consciousness they might lead us toward. This is the attitude we need to cultivate when forming relationships with either Stones or any other Symbols of spiritual significance.

Therefore there is no use merely touching our foreheads indifferently against the surface of any stone, feeling round it with our fingertips and expecting all sorts of information to come pouring out in vividly pictorial or other fashion. What we want we must go in and get for ourselves. There is no other real way of obtaining anything worthwhile. Until we learn how to do this in a spirit of love for the Life-forces connected with the stones or other materials in question, they will remain uncommunicative or merely misleading. Nothing but this one factor will really open them up.

It may not be possible to get blood from a stone, but we can obtain communication with life-levels having former or possibly future blood-ties with our world. To attempt this, it is only necessary to establish our physical contact with the stone, and then adjust our Inner attitude of awareness to attune with the objective we seek. It is far from easy to describe this adjustment in words, since it is worked without any. What are we looking for in this instance, anyway? Of equal importance is the question of *who* we are looking for. In this case, we are seeking contact with the collective and individual intelligences of whoever was once associated with these particular stones when living on earth, or whatever may still deal with them from discarnate states of being. These have to be approached in a spirit of faith, feeling, and friendship amounting to a sort of "cosmic comradeship" linking us with Life on all levels, whether past, present, or future. This was once called rather beautifully "loving kindness", and nothing less will serve us for this practice.

So, once the physical posture has been adopted, we must continue with the much more important arrangements of our Inner attitudes as we strive to grasp the intangible contents of the stone with something like the same certainty with which we can feel its surface with our fingertips. This means we have to arouse in ourselves a sincere sense of love and good-will for the spiritual principles we believe the stones stood for, and a definite personal feeling of friendship towards those people who were and are concerned with these same principles in association with this particular circle. Once we have evoked this Instate and brought it to a focal point in ourselves, we should then project it into, through, and beyond the symbol of the stone as far as we can toward the internal force-fields of its supra-physical structure. There should be no attempt whatever at "making pictures", or verbalising anything. Initially any such incidental impressions should be ignored or dismissed so far as possibly avoidable, no matter how interesting or tempting they may seem. The important thing is to keep entirely centred and concentrated along the pure theme of love-friendship contact which is appreciable through spiritual proximation alone. This is allied with the sense-certainty we obtain from the responsive pressure of friendly hands, the touch of loving lips, or whatever else conveys by contact only that we are actually in touch with an agent of our love-need. However, this attitude is arranged, it should be pushed through the stone toward the Inner objective with a firm and persistent pressure for quite an appreciable period until some responsive reaction is experienced.

There are only three types of response possible, which may be summed up roughly as pro, anti, and neutral. Their effects are quite clear to understand, and should determine whether or not to continue the experiment, or what further lines to take in connection therewith. In the case of an anti-reaction, something in the nature of a rejective barrier will be felt Inwardly, and a sort of instinctive antipathy be experienced almost spontaneously. It should not be assumed this derives from any evil influence, but ought to warn the recipient not to continue the contact without very adequate reason and sufficient personal protection in the way of knowledge and ability to cope with what the contact may bring up. A neutral response, of course, simply results in all our efforts sliding gently into a state of subsidence and apparent ineffectuality. When this happens, which may be frequently, it is wrong to suppose that no response whatever has been received. This is a very common mistake. Neutralisation of our offered energies actually is a form of Inner response to them. All it indicates is that they have been absorbed into some containing category of Cosmic consciousness. Anything or nothing may eventuate from them. Whether or not this satisfies us, at least it should leave the issue entirely open concerning whatever follow-up or otherwise we may decide upon. We should never be discouraged or disturbed in the slightest way by any neutral response we may receive. It should simply be counted as a "free try", well worth expenditure of energy for the sake of the practice and experience gained without penalties or undue payments. There is no mistaking the pro-reaction. It results in an augmentation and enhancement of our initial energies in such a way that we realise they are being implemented by reciprocals we are receiving from Inner sources outside our immediate self-supply. We know that something and someone from somewhere is responding favourably to our well-meant intentions because these increase as if by themselves, and seem to be reflected back at us with a sort of additional wave of acknowledgement. Our Inner instincts tell us we have received recognition from other levels of intelligent Life than our usual ones. This response may be so faint it is scarcely discernible, but nevertheless it can definitely be detected. Once we become accustomed to receiving and recognising it, there only remains the question of amplification and conversion into terms of consciousness we can reproduce for ourselves along more customary and ordinary lines. This part of the process, of course, takes place in our own personal circle of consciousness, and therefore is entirely limited by our own capabilities therein. It is all not unlike radio reception whereby an extraneous signal is detected and picked up, then amplified and converted to audio-frequency. If the set is inadequate the output will be poor, no matter how good the incoming signal was. To actually receive, and then convert an Inner signal into reasonable results of cognitive consciousness are two distinct parts of a programme. We need some degree of effectiveness in both if we are to sense out the stories certain stones have to tell us in their confidential circles.

At first, therefore, the essential part of the exercise consists of adopting a correct Inner attitude, projecting this through the selected stone or other focus, then recognising and appreciating the type of response received. There should be no attempt to go beyond these limits into audiovisual areas. What ought to be done instead, is follow the response if this seems favourable, by means of the Inner sense corresponding to touch in the physical sense-spectrum. This will bring in the essential basics out of which the rest may be built later. It is not more possible to describe the "hows" of this precise process than it is to tell anyone exactly how to see, hear, or smell anything. Every sentient soul has the faculty if they will only cultivate it. To see, one must first open the eyes, to hear properly the ears must be uncovered, to smell, the nostrils clear for incoming breath, and to touch we must approximate ourselves by body contact and estimate the nature of this by the type of sensation experienced. So to touch the non-physical part of anything, we have to simply put our Inner sentience as close to it as we can get and stay that way while we sort out whatever sensations we receive in return—if any. There is little else we can do, except gradually become more expert as we go along.

If we are only dealing with the metaphysical contents of a material actuality, why any necessity for physical contact? This fair question is often asked. The answer is because some practical means is needed for singling out any particular point of enquiry from all the rest, and also for obtaining a predominant "signal strength" from that source which will enable us to confine our consciousness within the limits of its especial information, so that signals from other sources do not "drown it out" or make it unintelligible. By far the easiest way of commencing this contact is by an ordinary touch-link. A real expert could gain this degree of contact without physical touch, but even then only by extending etherically in order to touch the objective along Inner levels. Extensions of this nature beyond reasonable limits outside immediate Self-circles are not without risks of discomfort and possible injury. The common or garden touch-contact is undoubtedly the "good old reliable."

There may be many instances, however, when immediate touch contact is either extremely difficult or entirely impossible. Especially for those with ageing bones and increasing inagility. In the old days they solved most of this problem with the aid of a plain ash-staff. With one end planted on whatever they were dealing with, and the other end held against their foreheads with both hands, they devoted their attention to the contact aimed for. Sometimes, when lost for ideas or asking for Inner help in general terms, they stuck one end of the staff straight in the ground, and bending their heads over joined hands held at staff-top, implored inspiration directly from Mother Earth herself, or anyone associated with her who cared to answer. Whether or not the staff acted as some kind of a real or symbolic aerial may be uncertain, but it is surprising how such a simple practice can still produce results in our times. To test it, the only necessity is to try it. A slightly more sophisticated version of this method is to cut a thin, light, and straight rod about three feet or less in length, terminating in as equal as possible a fork, the tines of this being left some eight inches or so long. The end of this rod is sharpened to a blunt-angled point. To use this divining-rod, the single end is placed against the object of contact, and the springy forked end held down by light pressure against the temples. The eyes are best closed, but if left open should be directed along the stick and the focus adjusted so that the image appears as two sticks crossed about centrally. This will induce just the right degree of auto-hypnosis needed to assist the operation of extended awareness. The projective process is then carried out in the customary manner. Sometimes with this system, a sort of "build-up" effect may actually be felt at one temple or the other, as if attention were being directed that way on purpose. Different types of receptives will interpret all these impressions in various ways, each according to the capacities of their consciousness. It does not follow that anyone will be specifically right or wrong in their variants, but only that their interpretations will depend on their capabilities of discernment and definition. All are of interest, and each has its value as part of a profound picture. It is most important that transference of energy from one Self-state to another via these stone media be made at as deep levels of consciousness as possible. This is one major reason why audio-visual impressions should not be sought initially. The idea should be to obtain a sort of "totality transfer" which will copy into the individual consciousness en bloc so to speak, sufficient of the Inner intelligence sought after to make subsequent self-selection from it possible with the greatest convenience and advantage. In a sense, this is like getting an instant picture which can be developed and selectively framed later, or transcribing a master-tape at high speed which may be rearranged and synthesised afterwards to give reasonable and acceptable results. It is all a question of "getting a good picture", or "taking a true tape" in the first instance. This is what we should aim for with all our Inner contacts via stones or other objective foci. In fact, our guiding motto might well be here, "Take true!" Once this has been done in moments or minutes, and the contact successfully conveyed to our personal stores of consciousness, we can keep constantly referring to it there, and gaining new information and enlightenment from it for as long as we like, while supplies last, which can be a very long time if we worked properly at first. This is almost as if we copied a whole book into our consciousness in a flash, then found ourselves set up with reading matter for years. The initiations of old were supposed to operated along this principle. Anyway, let us see what might be done with its use at the Rollrights.

CHAPTER TWO

A VISIT

To think about the Rollrights is one thing, but to visit them physically in search of what to think is quite another—especially when the only transport available is a bicycle and the Stones are twenty odd miles off across several toughish hills and dales. Nevertheless, when facts are looked in the face, what better means could there be in modern times for making what might be described as a "magical journey" or pilgrimage in connection with the past? Effort is the essence of any pilgrimage, and without that factor no really valuable Inner experiences are to be gained. Modern motors may have made it easy for us to reach important places, but they have totally deprived us of all the benefits obtainable otherwise. Who can possibly have any rewarding experience of a spiritual nature while sitting in or driving a noisy vehicle full of mechanical vibrations with an undercurrent of petrol fumes, not to mention the blare of pop music from the radio as well. The motorist's world is indeed a mad one of its kind.

It should also be remembered that an enclosed motorist is quite cut off from the Inner influences of the countryside which are so important in affairs of this nature. For one thing, visual contact with it is confined to the road and the hazards thereof, and for another, the speed of the vehicle makes mental contacts with the country impossible. It takes appreciable time to receive and reciprocate the spiritual solidities of any countryside, and to hear what it has to say we must be very, very quiet ourselves. These prerequisites prevent motorists from ever partaking in pilgrimages of this sort.

After all, the actual journey by which we arrive at a spiritually selected objective should be a most important part of the whole concern. Almost step by step there ought to be something to learn, something to undergo, and something to be gained inwardly in connection with the entire enterprise. Otherwise why bother to go anywhere? What good will any journey bring anyone if it has no Inner content worth considering? In old times, pilgrims enriched themselves spiritually not only from the places they went to, but also those they went through on the way. They had time to think, and varied experiences were revealed to them at a rate which made reflective ideation practically possible. This gave them the chance to alter themselves accordingly as they went along, and return with a much enhanced consciousness from the state of mind they commenced with. They changed consciousness *at depth*. Their modern motoring counterparts can only do so superficially. That makes all the difference between the two processes.

Apart from these considerations, it is quite obvious that in the old days people travelled farther than twenty something miles to their "Great gatherings" on solemn occasions. What is more, they had far tougher conditions to cope with than those imposed by any bicycle. Only the roughest of tracks, inadequate if any footwear, poor diet, dangers of wild beasts, in fact, dozens of disadvantages. Yet travel they did, and enrich themselves by the experience they must have done, or they would not have attempted it. Surely any average able-bodied fellow-traveller in this century might make a feeble attempt to follow those long-gone footsteps on a machine which, strictly speaking, only lengthens and speeds a natural stride somewhat.

We may get some slight idea of what these pilgrimages meant to the "old 'uns" from a so-called "Summons to a Sabbath", probably of late medieval origin, but drawn from far older traditions. It runs:

Ye shall come through brake and fen.
Ye shall come through thorn or forest,
Ye shall come over hill, down dale.
Ye shall come neither clothed nor naked,
Ye shall come neither walking nor flying.
Ye shall come neither in sun nor moon,
Ye shall come neither anointed or unanointed.
Ye shall come neither in haste nor sloth.

Sometimes the line "Ye shall come in Our Lady's Name" was added.

Such were the conditions imposed on would-be visitants to an old time Sacred Circle. Firstly we note the almost commando-like endurance of proceeding through bracken, marsh, hill climbs, and descent hazards. Then the specification that any form of ceremonial clothing would not be worn on the journey, but presumably carried in a pack. "Neither walking nor flying" implies that they might ride a beast if they chose, or else use "leaping sticks", which we would now call vaulting poles to help them get over obstacles like small streams or fallen tree trunks across a path. Coming neither in sun nor moon, indicated dusk as the best time for the exercise since this offered good chances for concealment in shadow while there was still enough light to move around. Neither anointed nor unanointed points to the practice of using hallucinogenic embrocation, or "lifting balm" as it was succinctly termed. This had to be only partially applied before the journey commenced, for it might prove dangerous if the travellers became so disoriented at the commencement that they fell into bogs, got lost on moors, or died of exposure. Therefore just a little of the stuff was rubbed in to begin with, and the amount absorbed slowly during the journey would help the remainder act rapidly when they arrived. Hence the last injunction to press on at a reasonable rate not too fast and exhaust the travellers, nor too slowly and arrive chilled and sluggish. All good practical instruction for the times and circumstances.

It is doubtful if the original Stone Circlers knew a great deal about hallucinogenic ointments, although they had other methods of getting their "lift-offs" from ordinary levels of living. Therefore, it was decided not to employ hallucinogenics in any ancient or modern form, though it must be confessed that a small amount of good Scotch whisky is not an unacceptable adjunct at the conclusion of such a long and tiring haul through the Cotswold countryside on chilly or clammy nights.

Why nights? For several reasons. First, because it is only in the early hours that one has much hope of catching the Rollrights by themselves, and sometimes not even then if caravans or cars pull into the little lay-by in front of them. This is a chance which has to be taken on almost any fine night of the year. Next, night time is about the last hope during our days for finding the countryside comparatively quiet and even communicative. In daytime every road is filled with roaring motors and petrol-fume pollution, to say nothing of the power mechanisms now in use on farms, such as mowers, saws, tractors, etc. On top of this literally are aircraft of all sorts with propellers, rotors, and jets carving the very air into cacophony. At least during the night most of these nuisances are abated to minimum.

The great advantage of a bicycle is its relative silence, and the fact of being so easy to get off and stay still at any given instant. It is also a considerable aid to thinking. While bodily muscles are involved with the mere mechanics of working the thing, the mind is able to rise relatively clear above the process and engage its efforts with constructive consciousness along other lines. Especially with slow speeds and reasonably clear roads at night, only a minimum of mental attention need be devoted to actually guiding the machine, while the remainder of one's awareness is occupied with the objectives behind the exercise.

Meanwhile, it is possible to keep in touch with all the invisible influences of the countryside which only seem evident at night, when they have more chance of reaching motor-muddled moderns. It is incredible how close and intimate such contacts sometimes seem, and the amazing amounts of Inner information they can bring those receptively attuned to their meanings. On a bicycle, one is free at any moment to stop and investigate some intriguing incident if it seems worth while. A handy and almost invaluable companion here is a cassette tape-recorder to store up all impressions and ideas at the time of their initial impacts. In that way, any trip may be practically re-lived subsequently, and every little item and incident commented upon recalled clearly to consciousness, together with thoughts since attached by subconscious workings. As a matter of interest, let us recapitulate the salients of one such trip and see just what emerged from it.

The time was early July and the weather hot, but with a N.E. air-stream, only the slightest wind perceptible, two days after full moon. Clear skies, rising ground-mist, journey began at 10.45 p.m. Uneventful for nearly the half hour needed to escape from built up areas. Then the unusual brilliance of a glow-worm appeared unexpectedly in a grass verge near the main road. These are rare in this vicinity, and especially just a solitary specimen advertising its presence hopefully in search of a mate. The brilliance of the little creature's three bands of light round its middle can scarcely be described. It was clearly seen from over twenty feet away. After it had been carefully examined and admired without interference, the journey was continued. Now, however, a whole train of thought had been commenced concerning the Three Rings of Cosmic Inner Light, and the faculty which humans should have for "turning on" their own illumination. That small grub certainly let loose some large thinking.

Next came the mists. Cotswold mists rise very oddly out of the ground and tend to drift round like dispossessed ghosts seeking sympathy. It is extraordinary how they seem to surround solitary travellers as if they really were semi-visible wraiths trying to attract attention. As they close in, one gets a most peculiar sense of being *accompanied* by some inexplicable type of intelligence. All the mists probably do is enhance that apprehension of "otherness" which is normally dormant during commonplace living. Nevertheless, they afforded a means of reacting with natural phenomena in order to alert the Inner areas of apperception which would be so much needed later on. They also helped to answer a problem. What happened in the long-ago time when similar or worse conditions threatened to prevent travellers from reaching their destination or might lead them to far worse fates? This question, pushed along the most available lines open, received an interesting reply.

Realising how children's voices carried for very far distances in still conditions, the old tribespeople trained youngsters to act as "hill-callers". There were characteristic cries which could be uttered so as to indicate the family, district, or other locatory information. Nearly everyone in a district was familiar with most of these calls, though some were taught as sacred secrets during initiatory instruction. This type of "hill-telegraph" could pass on quite comprehensible messages in sonic shorthand for those trained in its use. There were special calls for most needs. Some for greetings, some for help, others for warnings. The old people seem to have anticipated the Commercial Code by some thousands of years. The cries were even handed down through the ages from one generation of children to another until all their meaning was lost, and they either fell into total disuse or became "Fairy-tale" magic words supposed to make all sorts of things happen. So they did once, when people knew what they meant and acted on them. Some of them are still with us here and there today. As primitive foghorns, those young voices in the past must have guided many pilgrims through much more perilous paths, though, of course, they might also have led others into carefully contrived traps. Anyway, quite a number of minor issues became apparent with this latest information from "Inside."

As altitude was gained and mists thinned out, the blood-red rising moon could be seen in mysterious magnificence. It was a thrilling sight arousing inherent instincts reaching very far along genetic connections of Life-consciousness. There was "Our Lady" in whose Name a summons was once sent to those who still kept up her cult in secret. When the Rollright Circle was fairly new, however, most folk accepted Lady Luna quite naturally under different Names and took it for granted that those free to foregather in Circles celebrating her company would come when she shone so brightly to welcome them. It was a very old, old story being heard anew on this occasion. Somehow the Moon Maiden will never seem so silver-pure again now that Man has set his first dirty footmark on her face. The bloody disc still shamefully haunting the tree-lined horizon almost appeared to run red with the rape she had then so recently suffered.

With the gaining of physical heights came also a strangely marked sense of heightened Inner awareness and an increasingly keen appreciation of auto-existence. How obvious it seemed that so-called civilised humans are but somewhat less than half alive at the best of times. Here, everything was intensified and brought to a very fine point of balance indeed. There was an odd feeling of being watched from all angles. Not in any hostile way whatever, but simply out of interest in the strange mortal passing through the natural habitat of other lifelings. The countryside was calling in its secret speech which only those who know the sound of silence can recognise. Once a reply had given the password in the same tongue, a reciprocal appreciation of Life in the whole locality extending everywhere else was experienced. The life of the land, and a living human being had met on common terms of metaphysical consciousness, and each had recognised their relationship together. It is a unique understanding beyond verbal approaches to the Verities of Life.

What is so difficult to explain is the extraordinary enhancement of a general Life-sense which comes with these conditions. Vitality abounds amazingly, and so does sensitivity. It becomes suddenly clear how much sharper and keener were the investigatory instincts of early Man in his natural environs than our socially stifled sensoria in the pseudo-surrounds we have set up to gratify our greeds. Here, in the middle of the night on top of the Cotswolds, we realise at last just how effective our forebears were with eyes, ears, and noses. The very slightest and most insignificant stimulus had to be located, identified, and classified for conscious action with far greater speed and precision than any modern computer can yet attain. Life itself might depend on correct decisions. Moreover, there is an important Inner consideration involved. Our physical senses and their super-physical counterparts extend into each other and can be consciously followed in either direction. That is to say, if we were sufficiently sensitive we should be able to "smell down" any odour until it became too faint for physical sensors to continue with further, then by a process of Inner adjustment extend our psycho-sensory equipment along the same line in search of more information from other dimensions of existence. The same, of course, applies to the other senses. It is only when we are able to focus and sharpen them very finely indeed that we can increase their depth of penetration sufficiently to realise something of what lies behind ordinary living levels. There is nothing like solitary communion with the Life-Spirit, available maybe most readily in conditions of a moon-lit countryside at a fair altitude, for bringing one face to face with such conclusions.

So far, all the experience encountered along this particular journey led to a steadily improving sense of Inner sensitivity and appreciation. Of course, the stress and fatigue factor began to exert its influence after fifteen or so miles of ups and downs. A not uncorpulent corpus propelling itself along with considerable effort after mid-life point has been passed is bound to show signs of stress-sensitisation. Providing this can be guided into controlled courses of consciousness, very valuable use may be made of it for brief periods of Inner investigation. That was the reason for former practices known as "watching and praying", now well-known as stress-sensitisers of the psyche.

The remainder of the trip to the Rollrights went more or less to schedule. There was one wonderful glide for six solid miles down a road which would have to be tramped up again next day under a scorching sun, but who cared about that when the Moon-Lady called so clearly and sweetly from a serene sky. Several stiff climbs and short runs later, the last leg of a two mile reasonably level road to the Rollrights was reached. It is a curious psychic phenomenon, but there seems to be a sort of "power-perimeter" round the Circle approximately a mile from its centre. At any rate, there is a definite point where the influence of the Stones is unmistakably "picked up", and from there it is almost like homing in on a radio beacon. Arriving at the Stones themselves compares with finding a whole crowd of friends assembled to greet someone most welcome among them. There they were, all their familiar faces seeming to smile in the happiest possible style. Was it pure fancy caused by exhaustion only, or did the Stones really do a little dance in the magnificent moonlight? The Twelve were certainly dancing in the Heavens at that moment. On Earth, one mortal with slightly sore feet and a sensitive stern joined their company with a firm, though friendly, intention of sitting the next dance out.

It was a truly magical atmosphere. At three in the morning under a brilliant moon with a soft summer scent in the surprisingly mild and invigorating air, almost anything wonderful might happen. It did. Not a single motor passed for the remainder of the night and no sound whatever broke the speaking of the Stones till some time after dawn when they had said all they would on that occasion, anyway. Only those who also know the Stones are likely to realise how very rare is such a prolonged peaceful period, especially during a summer season. That alone was an amazing experience. Granted such a grace, it only became necessary to follow the silence straight inside itself until the voices of the Stones became clear enough to carry on a conversation. From Stone to Stone around the Circle, stopping to talk with one or the other on the way as old friends will, another collection of "inside information" came across from one circle of consciousness to another.

What did the Stones say? Did they tell all kinds of stellar secrets or reveal high Mysteries of Magic, or mention far-off Masters from other

The Stone Circle

planets who set them up for the benefit of this one? Nothing of the kind at all. They spoke of the simplest and smallest things that linked them with Life on very fundamental levels indeed. Commonplace to them, but new and interesting for learning human inner ears. For some reason on this particular visit the Stones mentioned a good deal about some of the crafts and skills their setters were familiar with, although previously unrealised by the listener. Such as the particular way they pinned skins together in order to make garments, or fixed skins to wooden frameworks while they were still wet, so that as they dried out in the sun while carefully weighted with small stones, the structure pulled tightly together and became a shield, carrying tray, or other receptacle, depending on shape. As shields, these articles were most useful, because they were so light to carry for long distances and, if properly drum-like would bounce quite largish stone missiles from their surfaces. They were also used for making drum signals which could be heard quite far away by sharp ears undeafened by civilised clamour.

Not that the Stone-setters considered themselves in any way uncivilised. To the contrary, the Stones stand today as memorials of human culture and civilised customs. They were placed by a people familiar with laws, language, codes and conventions, and an entire social structure from which our own descended into its present dubious condition. Those people built up a complete civilised association with each other because of a Life-attitude they shared with Life itself. They were not savages growling and snarling as they snatched scalding meat from each other or beat women with huge hambones. Doubtless on occasion their individual behaviour might be as bad and maybe worse than ours, but basically the original Stone-setters had reached certain conclusions in connection with Cosmos which led them together into the common Life-Circle their Stones stood for. In fact, the very phrase "to stand for" signifies a marker Stone having an inherent meaning. Crude as their civilisation was, contrasted with our present complexities, those old Stone-setters had reached an Inner state of spiritual solidity we may well afford to envy from our shaky standpoints of uncertainty in these times.

Each Stone approached for the next hour or so had something to say for itself which made sense, but it was mostly communicated through quite simple symbols. Line-patterns, for instance, and hand movements expressive of mind-motives. They all seemed somewhat anxious to convey the definite message that the Stones had been set up in a spirit of friendly companionship and intended to stay like that as long as they could. In their own way they said: "If we could do it, why not ye?" That there always would be arguments and disputes among Mankind they knew well enough, but they also realised all arguments could be settled properly inside a special Circle constructed for that purpose among others. If it had worked for them in their way, they reasoned, why might not we, their distant descendants, do much the same in our days. How possible to explain in reply what any modern mortal should be ashamed to admit— we neither trust nor love each other enough to make Circles capable of containing our effective living community. The Stones considered this carefully, and then supposed that if sufficient people got together in small Circles all over the world it would add up into a big enough bond to include everyone. So indeed it might, but what intelligent individual of today has faith enough in his fellows to believe anything like this possible for one instant? There seemed no point in arguing this out with a Stone on such an otherwise convivial occasion, so conversation returned to lighter levels.

The surrounding silence was rather beautifully broken by birds beginning their delightful dawn chorus. Although it wanted nearly an hour to actual daybreak, these lovely little heralds of the sun began to warn the moon her spouse was approaching for their momentary meeting. Somehow the Stone Circle seemed a rather wonderful sort of wedding ring to link the Luminaries into a mystical marriage lasting as long as Life itself. For the instant of sunrise, it became necessary to join the group of welcoming watchers known as the "Whispering Knights", standing by themselves in the shadows at the far edge of a field to the East of the Circle.

These four remaining Standers, with their fallen comrade capstone, are much more solemn than the Circlers as a rule, but they appeared relatively cheerful in this instance. Once, they said, there were seven of them supporting the capping central Stone raised between Heaven and Earth by the intervention of Man. They stood for the Ways of Wisdom or, as we might say, the "Pillars of the Principles". They upheld what they understood. Together, we could consider them as "Counsellors" or advisers concerning human affairs in connection with Cosmos. They certainly seemed most benevolent and even jocular on this majestic morning. Almost like seniors unbending in a mellow mood toward a minor member of their family.

There are one or two small items of ceremony to observe in company with the Counsellors, and these very simple symbolic acts were duly done. The Stones grew solemn again, and as dawn came close, they spoke of new light on old things keeping the Cycle of Life going round Circles of Consciousness forever. They summoned everyone alive to put their heads together with good will like themselves, in order to support a common burden of Being beneath the sun. That was the only practical way to share the weight of wisdom, they said. So for a brief while, a human head was laid alongside theirs in consultation with collective consciousness attainable by anyone able to meet other minds apart from their physical presence. The Counsellors "stand in" for most of Mankind, especially those in empathic companionship. Then all looked for Light.

The sun was born that day as we are—in blood. It even appeared between two Counsellors behind a tree as if it were in the act of issuing from an opening womb. There was the Tree of Life between two Pillars, bearing the Sign of Life bathed in that Royal Blood which is the true Holy Grail or Sangreal. Confronted by such a mighty Mystery, only one acknowledgement was acceptable. Sincerely humble homage to the Living Spirit so powerfully portrayed. This was most gladly given, and the hope of its reception held in heart. Now, the Sun being risen in regal splendour, was the moment to join its representative on Earth at the King Stone.

This monolith has a most interesting face which can be seen most clearly at dawn when light comes from a low angle. The actual face is just rising out of the earth in left profile, while the remainder of the Stone

The Whispering Knights

above it is a huge headgear not unlike that of ancient priest-kings. The face is mild and benevolent, with a well kept beard and soft, down-flowing moustaches. A face to be trusted by the look of it. Its general expression might be described as calmly composed and confident. These features, of course, are entirely due to the weathering of the Stone, but it is strange how they express exactly the feeling that contact with the Stone brings. Its Keyword is essentially, "Peace".

From behind the King-Stone that morning, the golden-red sun levelled in an azure sky with a silvering moon. The sun kept counsel with the Whisperers, and the moon hovered gracefully over the Stone Circle. Birds still sang strongly, and all around the King-Stone was a sea of green barley counter-charged by blazons of poppies. Once more the symbolic Sacred King was shedding Blessed Blood upon the people of this Earth. The signs of this ageless sacrifice were evident everywhere. It was a magical moment to be remembered for the remainder of a lifetime. All was *alive* to a point where sheer existence became almost excruciating, and one learns that Heaven may hurt as much as Hell. The pain of pure Beauty can be an exquisite experience.

By an odd chance, the flat stone embedded in the ground immediately back of the King-Stone rocked slightly when trodden on. This recalled old legends of rocking stones proclaiming rightful kings with a curious cry. Such a noise was indeed heard to some small degree, but it was caused by suction as the stone moved in its depression underfoot. Nevertheless, it added another mite of magic to the symbolic scenery. The King-Stone had little to say in particular, beyond a reminder to take spiritual responsibilities seriously and always uphold basic beliefs in Life. He did point out that he stood principally for the loyalty any Circle of companions should have among its members and toward whatever spiritual standards they shared together. So long as that loyalty remained unbroken, the Circle was safe, but once betrayed by a single deliberate act of anyone, the power of a whole Circle would be lost unless an excluding closure might be made. Kingship, he remarked, really meant the right rulings everyone must make for themselves, and that was why he stood alone independently of the Circle and Counsellors. There was more he would say on some future occasion. Now, with his blessing, the Circle might find room for another guest.

At breakfast time on that gloriously sunlit morning at the Round Table of the Rollrights somewhere about 6 a.m., the company seemed almost absurdly cheerful. Some Stones assumed all sorts of strange shapes in quite a carnival spirit. Their laughter was nearly audible to physical ears. They were echoing a faint fraction of former convivialities and celebrations which had occurred in their hearing during their centuries of human and associated companionship. This was an opportunity for wandering round the Circle informally while sending out currents of conscious energy along the lines certain Stones opened up. Absent friends, incarnate and otherwise were thought about and sent "wish-you-were-here" mental messages. Definite thinkings were directed into a few of the Stones so that at least the gist of these might be picked up by future visitants to some extent. Altogether, the Circle acted as a cyclotron of consciousness, giving and taking thoughts and ideas with increasing mental momentum.

It became clearly recognised while the now warmly shining sun dried out the remaining damp from dew-soaked clothing, that we live surrounded by Circles of Consciousness constructed by others just as this old Stone Circle was made. We are constantly ringed round by "thought perimeters" put up in the past and present by other people's minds, intentions, and structured thinking. This may be either a bad or a good thing for us, depending on how we relate ourselves therewith, but until each of us learns how to set up our own spiritual Circles around the Divine Spark we bear at the secret centre of our beings, we shall have to give and take what we may from the larger Life-Circles confining our consciousness to whatever set of circumstances are eventuating immediately in our vicinity.

So very much had been gained from the Stones during this single session alone, and much more had been taken in on deep storage levels for subsequent translation into focalised thought-force. In fact, there was such a mass of material to take home, it was a wonder the load on the machine felt no heavier on the return journey. Could consciousness be weighed, no cycle made in this world would ever have carried the increased amount added in this instance. Yet there was definitely an extra burden to take back intangibly. The weight of words on tape, the load of light on camera-film and, bulkiest of all, the mass of ideas on the mind. All these extras were indisputably real, and no one would doubt their existence. Why, therefore, should so many humans deny the actuality of an Awareness around them always, yet which is too Great for confinement within any circles we can define on Earth?

Eventually the passing of an early milk lorry announced with a raucous rattle that all good times must surely come to a fair conclusion. It seemed slightly sad to realise how horrid humanity sounds most of the time. When, if ever, are we likely to make motors sounding as beautiful as bird song, or looking as lovely as the countryside they despoil while tearing through it? How can a concrete-caged civilisation ever free itself from the captivities of consciousness it appears so anxious to adopt as life-limits? There are so many queries arising in our modern Circles which we seem unable to answer with any sense of satisfaction. Why should we be so clever in some directions yet so stupid in others? Is it because we live unevenly instead of trying to construct our consciousness in equable Circles around central Ideas of Identity? Whatever we may suppose, it is positively certain that we have indeed a lot to learn of Life yet before we become fit to enter any higher Circles of Consciousness. Sometimes, if lessons seem difficult to grasp, it pays to go right back to their fundamental principles again and find what might have been missed which would have made subsequent stages plain and simple. Hence, an occasional contact with our original Circle-patterns can be most helpful to muddled moderns.

Once collections of ideas start gathering around a central power-point in Circles, they begin building up into spiritual structures we can actually live in and work with. An assembly of such a kind gradually grew up in the course of many visits to the Rollright Circle like the one described. They did not all follow the same lines by any means. Quite different sorts of contacts were made on widely differing occasions. Eventually, an overall pattern appeared to be emerging which began to seem good spiritual sense. Ultimately, sufficient Inner intelligence enabled the summated Truth-total to be symbolically ritualised into fundamental realisations covering the Cosmic design behind all the Circle stood for, not only locally, but as a Way of Life to be continued throughout the whole of creation.

The major difficulty lay in aligning ancient and modern outlooks at Life into a timeless tie-up with Truths that are Cosmically changeless. This meant that any Inner inspiration assisting the collation of such consciousness would have to come from the same source which motivated men to construct these Stone Circles in the first place, long before they themselves realised the spiritual significance of what they were doing. In other words, there had to be a directing Intelligence somewhere behind the building of these Circles which was intentionally moving mankind toward the metaphysical realities they represented. If what was put together in the past was also for the sake of where it should lead in the future, then surely the Circles not only had meaning for modern man, but must still have their part to play for our coming conditions of living in this world or anywhere else.

In order to deal with consciousness covering such extents of Cosmos, we need some overall system of symbolism which is more or less universally acceptable. The basic symbol of any Circle is the simple Cross-Pattern of Life, or four-fold cycle of force. Sun-up to sunset marked one meridian, and right-angular associations of Winter–Summer marked the other. During early periods, Stone Circles were not particularly arranged to mark out Cosmic clocks or elaborate astronomical calculations. The Rollrights are earlier than Stonehenge, and have only a general orientation. We must not forget that first and foremost the Stones stood for people, and the most important people wanted the best places, which would naturally be to windward of the central fire so that smoke and sparks blew away from them. This again would mainly depend on prevailing winds, which in the Rollright area seems mainly S.W. So we must look at the Stones as a psycho-social structure appropriate for its day and situation. To learn something of this, information supplied by the Stones themselves along Inner lines will be used. This may not always be exactly in agreement with purely archaeological specifications, but at least nothing seems to clash very seriously with what is already known. It is the unknown areas of exploration which are likely to be of greatest interest in the specialised field we are about to cover.

CHAPTER THREE

THE GROUNDS OF BELIEF

Notwithstanding many highly interesting ideas, the far-back origins of a Stone Circle stem simply from a number of humans gathered round a fire or cooking place, each one marking his particular position with a suitable stone. Just as today we keep seats in a bus, train, or plane by leaving a paper, garment or luggage-item as a stand-in during an absence, so did our forebears claim their rightful places at the "food-warmth" centre around which tribal life circulated. This was the same pattern as Cosmos itself. Sun in the centre and planets going round it through the Zodiac. Not that the tribesmen realised this at the time. They only knew their gathering felt right when arranged in such a manner. So they kept their Circles going wherever they wandered, and as they expanded with experience of living and developed more evolved complexities of consciousness, their Circle-designs altered according to their changed social and cultural circumstances.

To understand this, it is necessary to look through the eyes of someone living in a very early Stone Age society. Where Fire, Food, and Friendship met, there was a Good Spirit in the middle of it all. They did not have to think this out in any theological way. They could feel it for themselves just as certainly as they felt warmth from the Fire, tasted succulence with the Food, and enjoyed companionship with the Friendship. If they could have used modern words to give their Spirit a name, it would most probably have been something like "Satisfaction" or "Safety". It is an ironic thought in passing that their modern counterparts have a similar God called "Social Security". With Stone Age society, as today, the most important factors of Life were safety, food, comfort, sex, and amusement. Whatever made people "feel good". In those days such fulfilments were not very frequent occurrences, but the most likely common denominator calculated to bring them together was undoubtedly the camp cook-fire.

Fire is the major factor in the ascendancy of Man above other animals on this Earth. Our entire evolution has depended on our handling of this Element. During the Stone Age, Fire brought power to the people in the same way that power has come to us with its Nuclear offspring in our Plastic Age. We use cyclotrons to control our sort of Fire, and they used Circles of Stone to keep theirs in bounds. The same problem presented to

Man from one Age to another. Our entire future may hang on just how much we have learned from the past. That is the relevance which Stone Circles should have for us in the present.

Given a good fire, Stone-Age Man could set up in the business of living for himself and his family quite well for his times. A fire frightened away wild animals which would be otherwise dangerous, cooked his food, straightened his spears, kept him warm, dried him when wet, and served him in many valuable ways providing it was kept in proper order and under control. It could easily kill very painfully if it got out of hand. Not much intelligence was needed to discover the advantage of surrounding a fire with sizable stones which contained it successfully. Nor did it take long to work out that the best place to be on chilly damp nights with perhaps only scanty leather clothing for covering, was in a circle round the precious fire where remnants of food were still reachable, and friendly faces might be reassuringly recognised. The problem always arose, however, just who sat or slept where.

Naturally, the most powerful and influential members of the family, clan, or tribe, always insisted in having the best positions. They still do. Quarrels, disputes, accidents, and even killings must have been almost incessant on this account in early times. They have not exactly stopped ever since. Looking back, it is not difficult to re-enact the events likely to occur when a whole pack of people are huddled round their fires and several latecomers arrive empty handed, ill-tempered and hungry, trying to force their way close to the food and fire. Those already there refuse to move away. Rude remarks about unskilled hunters deserving no meat are heard. It only needs one hasty blow to start faction-fights everywhere. Someone falls in the fire and dies of burns later. Worse still, the fire itself is nearly extinguished in the scrimmage, and several of the best hunters get their feet so badly burned they will be unable to provide food for their families for quite a while. Altogether a disaster for all concerned. Every human grouping in those far-off days must have experienced events of this kind to intolerable degrees of endurance. We do the same these days somewhat differently, but otherwise the fundamentals seem uncomfortably familiar.

We shall never know who was the first man, probably driven to desperation, who had the bright idea of marking his particular place by the fire with some special stone and defying anyone else to touch it. Whoever he was, he must have been fairly skilled or strong, or in some way highly respected and perhaps feared by the others. Most likely he was their leader, and made his point perfectly plain by saying, in effect,

"See this stone? It means me, and I'm putting it right here until I return. Whoever interferes with it does the same with me, and I'll smash his face in with this rock when I get back. Any questions?" There were probably no comments except a chorus of growls round the fire from other stalwarts agreeing while they quickly edged in on the act with stones of their own. The first closed shop in the world was in session.

It would not have taken long for the less stalwart but wide awake clan members to follow suit with wider stone rings round the first. Even the dimmest wit among them could not fail to notice the difference this new arrangement made to the social structure of the clan as a whole. Despite the creation of privileged positions, once everybody knew just where they were supposed to fit round the all-important Fire, a much more peaceful and constructive atmosphere among the people who were now classified into various circles. Just as the stones round the fire kept its destructive properties under proper control by placement, so did the stones round the people keep their worst propensities more or less within bounds. The Cosmos of civilisation had supervened over the Chaos of sheer savagery—up to a point, anyway.

The general idea obviously caught on within only a few generations of humanity, except maybe with minorities having what we would now call anti-social inclinations. Those who preferred fitting themselves in with the new circular schemes of society really began to prosper quite surprisingly. All that had actually happened was that once freed from constant quarrelling and inflicting injuries on each other, their relative social security gave them opportunities to develop natural skills and exchange the products of these with each other. Moreover, each class of circle began to realise the definite functions of the others. Probably those on the outskirts did feel resentful of the tough types hogging all the heat in the middle, but if the camp should be attacked by marauding beast or hostile humans, who had to grab blazing brands from the fire as quickly as possible and fight off the danger? Only the warrior-hunters were useful here. No one else was likely to deny these defenders their rights to a fireside place determined by their own particular stones.

Yet warriors alone would not keep the clan together in the numbers they now realised afforded them all their best chances of living. Somebody had to pass on skills to the young, and even entertain the community. Grudgingly or otherwise, brawn made place for brain, and courage had to admit cunning. Nor was a place on the council purely a male prerogative. Senior females soon asserted their matriarchal authority and disciplined the tribal daughters from the central circle, which now had grown rather wider and more representative of the clan as an entire people. The stones had grown as well, and by this time were mostly big enough to sit on, and occupied permanent places round the central Fire of most established encampments. Even today we talk about a "seat" belonging to any member of a governing body. Not only did these stone "seats" represent their owners, but they also became stylised according to social status. The most important people insisted on having the biggest and best stones to suit their self-esteem, nor would they tolerate mere rank and file tribal members sporting a better class of stone than theirs. Conventions and styles with stones arrived fairly early on the scene, and are still with us in principle. It may be significant that the slang term for diamonds is "rocks".

Also early in Circle civilisation came the convention of family and hereditary holdings. People began assigning the rights over their personal stones to their heirs who were acceptable to the rest of the clan. This also meant they kept wealth of power or property in the family. Whether or not they ever sold or transferred their stone-rights to someone quite outside their circles is very uncertain, but the strong probability is this would not be possible without clan consent. Then, as now, the bulk of humanity were mainly content to let their leaders make decisions for them and take on the responsibilities of running the general affairs of a whole clan or tribe. Competition for the stone seats of privilege might not have been so fierce as could be supposed. The chances are that hereditary positions were handed down through very many generations before original linkage got broken, and even then fresh appointments would carry on old titles and names.

As generations succeeded each other, more and more importance became attached to the stones signifying their place in society. It became considered that those stones actually held all the departed ancestral spirits associated with them. In a way this was true. Sensitives able to interpret influences imparted to particular stones by long dead people would quite naturally assume those identical people were still speaking, and issuing advice from the Otherworld, which to that extent was so. Certain stones seemed to have more in them than others, and those were regarded with particular reference, not to say almost awe for the Great Unseen—though not unfelt. If a special stone felt unusually charged with meaning it would be reserved for rulers. Later on, such "spirit-stones" were further classified, and two good examples in use even today are the Coronation Stone in Westminster Abbey, and the Archiepiscopal "Seat of Augustine" in Canterbury Cathedral.

After probably several millennia of human lifetimes, all kinds of codes, customs, and concentrations became firmly associated with stones both in and out of their Circles. By then they had grown up into imposing collections and groupings of a multilithic nature. The Circles grew as large as the combination of local families whose Stones composed them. Those Stones were now much more than mere little lumps of rock anyone could carry around from place to place wherever they went. Once a whole tribe of people had settled themselves into an area, they felt the need of a substantial civic Circle which would adequately represent their cultural and social advancement. Big and important families demanded big and important stones to indicate their position among the people. It took the able-bodied men of that family an enormous amount of effort to procure and set up Stones they considered worthy of their status, but eventually they accomplished the task to their satisfaction. Smaller families had to be content with smaller stones, but the consideration was to get a Stone in a Circle at all. By this time, many Circles were getting more exclusive than modern clubs. Unless people got themselves attached in some way to a particular Stone by blood-ties, marriage adoption, or similar convention, they had no rights within that Circle except as visitors or for some other well recognised reason.

Each Stone forming a Circle stood for definite people living in that particular area, together with their relatives alive or dead, and indicated how those people fitted into the community from a social standpoint. Any intelligent man of those times could take one look round a stone Circle and more or less guess what sort of folk had set it up. Though they had no alphabets to read, they did have symbols in the shapes and sorts of Stones which stood for certain types of people. This Stone, for instance, showed the wealthiest and most influential people in the place. That one stood for a small family whose speciality was basket making. Another over there meant a fairly important lot who owned a pottery business. Then several very ordinary and average citizens who were nevertheless worth including in the civic Circle. A stranger to any area in those days would know at once what the locals were like from the Circle they had set up for themselves. To see the Stones was to see the people, their ancestors, and even recognise the particular Spirit which kept them together. Both Stones and people were related by a common code of consciousness. We should do well by remembering this when visiting Stones in our times.

If a full tribal assembly were called into the Circle, all members would stand by their own Stones while the leaders and elders held the centre stations. Contrary to popular supposition, these gatherings were mainly not for religious rites or reasons at all, but principally for social, political, commercial, or cultural purposes. Religion, *per se*, had not at that time separated very much from the ordinary affairs of living, and was such an essential part of existence that almost anything and everything could constitute an act of relationship with the Life-Spirit. This is positively something we need to re-discover along modern lines. Nevertheless, there had evolved a species of worship in a way which was something akin to Shaman practice insofar as it called for a specialist or specialists in making deeper than average contacts with the "Inworld" or "Spiritstate". These individuals, male or female, were mostly the "odd ones out" among any mass of mankind who have an inherent instinct for sensing something of what lies behind and beyond the usual areas of awareness available to most mortals. Much later, Celts were to call this faculty simply "the Gift", and everyone knew what was meant. In early times every clan depended on at least one such member capable of giving guidance to the rest. Very often this person was a woman, and sometimes quite elderly for those days, being even upward of thirty or so!

In well established communities, such as the Rollright confederation, the Circle served as a forum, market, tribunal, theatre, assembly-place, and general public meeting ground. It also served as a fortified enclosure in emergency since it was defensively palisaded, although this was not its chief function. First and foremost, it was intended to be the centre of local civilisations and a common point where members of included families might deal peacefully and profitably with each other for the sake of better living all round. Here also they could meet others from different tribes or lands, and do business and pleasure together. Call it an Exchange, a Capitol, or better still a Round Table, for this was the forerunner of Arthurian and other chivalric Codes, but however the early Stone Circles are termed, they were most certainly places where all the principles of modern civics came from. When we enter them today, we should do so with recognitive respect on that account.

To each individual member of a Circle, the "family Stone" or "Old One" had a depth of spiritual significance very hard for us to understand now. That particular Stone stood for all they ever were or would be. It would not be correct to say that an ancestral Stone meant as much to its Circle members as a "family seat" does now to a titled owner. The Stone meant very much more than that. It not only offered status in this world, but was the gateway to the spirit world also. In it lived every ancestor. If an ear was pressed closely to the Stone when the countryside was fairly silent, those Otherworlders might be heard whispering good counsel or warnings to their living descendants. No use listening at someone else's Stone to learn his secrets. Only family spirits spoke to blood-links with Life. That was the Law. Of course, there were special Stones which spoke to the people periodically, but only those "in the know", or Wise Old Ones could make those talk.

Here, an interpolation is necessary to clear up an unfortunate misunderstanding which has been encroaching into our language during the past few years. It concerns the misuse and wrong interpretation of the Anglo-Saxon word "Witch" (see Appendix). There has arisen a kind of loose assumption that the term derives from a root "Wicca", meaning the "Craft of the Wise". In fact, "Wicca" (male) and "Wicce" (female), means nothing of the sort whatever. Wic is a stem signifying weak, from which derives "wicked", in the sense of something wrong, bad, evil, anti-social, etc. etc. In plain Anglo-Saxon, a Witch was fundamentally an evil and dangerous person to be dealt with accordingly. Witch and Wicked go together. It is even incorrect to speak of a "White Witch". One might as well say "White Black". It is most likely this error comes from inadequate etymological checkbacks. The correct Anglo-Saxon term for "Wise" is "Wita", a similarly sounding word. For example —"Witanagemot", the "Meeting of the Wise Ones". Modern misuses of the word "Witch" are apt to be laughable or pathetic depending on viewpoint. In a way, it does seem a little sad to note sincere and somewhat sinless pagan people of our times so anxious to proclaim themselves under a totally misunderstood title signifying a state of human ill-nature quite foreign to their kindly and well-meaning spiritual selves. All because of a literary error allowed to proliferate carelessly, chiefly on account of its sales value in sensational journalism. Any public reference library has the source-material to establish the rights and wrongs of this issue, which has something of an important bearing on the present point.

The crux of this matter is that claims or assertions are very likely to be made that the people of the Stone Circles were practitioners of some "Witch" cult, "craft", or other associative form of activity. If we put the word "Witch" in its proper place as indicative of ill-wishing and evil-doing, this is tantamount to an accusation against the Stone Circle people which they cannot refute except through minds and mouths defending them in our times. Whatever they were, they had no generic term for their specifically spiritual Life-attitudes which we might now term "religious". They were no more "Witches" than ordinary folk are today. On the whole, they wished each other well, not ill, and their "Wise" people were concerned with beneficent fertility, whereas the definition of a "Witch" was one who called the curse of sterility on man and beast alike. "Wise" ones were pro- and "Witches" anti-Life. Stone-Circlers firmly evicted or executed anyone among them unwise enough to call curses and evoke evil in their midst. They were human enough to hurl imprecations against common enemies, but if they found an enemy in their midst they dealt with that danger drastically. Their definition of a "Witch" would have been someone who turned against or betrayed those in whose Circle that wicked one belonged by birth, blood, or belief. A stab-in-the-backer, or someone who deliberately broke the belief-Circle of faith and trust in each other which all knew was so essential to established human living on earth. Someone likely to bring death and destruction upon fellow beings who were trying to keep humanity alive and purposeful upon this planet. Someone they virtually had to kill if they meant to remain healthy themselves. They would look at "Witches" like active anti-bodies look at an invading virus in an otherwise good bloodstream.

What we should realise if we can from our overcrowded civilisation, is how small and compact those Circle-communities were. Maybe a few hundred people only in some cases, mostly inter-related, and with a defensively corporate sense of survival. In social Circles of that kind, one single mischief maker alone can work amazing amounts of evil affecting everyone. It took only one person to extinguish the vital fire, put poisonous berries in a communal cooking-pot, or commit some anti-social act endangering the entire clan. The smaller the Circle, the greater the responsibility of its members toward each other. Large Circles are capable of absorbing and neutralising a certain quantity of ill-doing, but an act which might only annoy a big community could be fatal in the case of a small one. Yet in both instances the same underlying principles would apply.

Those old Stone-Circlers realised perfectly well how dangerous a "Witch", or someone intentionally antagonistic to their Life-pattern was, if allowed to continue in practice among them. To put ourselves in their place, let us suppose one member of an astronautical team "went bad" on the others while in the confining circle of a Space craft. The fellow crew-members literally could not afford to allow this menace to continue in living consciousness among them. For the sake of their own lives and the whole mission, they would simply have to kill or neutralise their dangerously defective companion. Not a sensible person on Earth would doubt the wisdom of such an act, or condemn those responsible. Let us at least credit communities of long ago with a sense of similar survival procedures. This was probably why stoning to death became the capital punishment method of executing those considered "social criminals". They had broken the sacred code of the Stones, so it was only justice that stones should slay them. Also, since they had acted against the entire tribe or clan, everyone ought to share responsibility for putting them to death. Condemnation was thus unanimous.

Therefore, to consider the Wise ones of old as any sort of "Witches" is both inaccurate and meaningless. It is high time this word was replaced in our language where it rightly belonged in the first instance, and evaluated for its authentic etymological content. If such an expression as "Craft of the Wise" is permissible, then this should properly be "Wise-craft", or even "Wit-craft", but on no account "Witch-craft", or the "Craft of the Wicked". The old Stone-Circlers may have been crude by some of our standards, but they were no more wicked than we are. Cynics might not suppose so much.

By and large, the Rollright Circlers were hard-working law-abiding citizens of their place and period. They had come a long way from purely primitive conditions of tribalism and barbarity which prevailed among their forgotten forebears, whose spirits had faded back into the Stone they sprang from. These people made clothing, ornaments, weapons, had herds, lived in shelters, and traded together with other tribes. On higher levels they had evolved definite codes of conduct, basic beliefs in their own social and spiritual significance which amounted to a Tradition, and were growing into objective approaches toward the Spirit of Life Itself, which eventually condensed into distinctly religious procedures. Since they did not write or read in our definition of those words, their Tradition was oral, passed down "from mouth to ear" from one generation to another. A lot of it was everyday instruction, some of it consisted of semi-secret skills "kept in the family", and very special items of information or ideas were reserved for the "high-ups" of the hierarchy who by now were descending from hereditary lines of ancestry which later produced the Priest-Kings of Biblical days. In other words, the pattern of the Circles had begun to reflect an Inner arrangement of Awareness which seemed to derive from Man's instinctive attempts in the general direction of Divinity.

We might not think very highly of those "special secrets" nowadays. We have outgrown them a long while back, though we shall never outgrow the principles behind them. Every generation of Mankind gains some new germs of "wider wisdom" which are secret insofar as relatively few human minds are consciously capable of compassing them. After some generations have passed by, those same rare realisations sink into the collective consciousness and emerging through genetic gates become what we call common knowledge. Originally, they were "Seed-ideas" implanted into the depths of human intelligence from a source of "Universal Awareness" entirely outside our ordinary Circles of consciousness altogether. In childlike terms; God planted a Seed of Light in the Dark Mind of Man, rather like a man planted a seed of Life in the dark womb of Woman. Once implanted, Man had to grow the seed-idea within him until it was ready to emerge into ordinary conditions of living and thinking. This was just like the way every creature had to grow inside its mother until it became big and strong enough to assume independent actions on its own account. What is so highly important here, is that if women were not fertilised by men there would be no more humans, and if human intelligence was not impregnated by a spiritual Seed-Source there would be no more advances of Awareness for Mankind. This was the foundation of the "Fertility Faith" held by the old Wise Ones, and handed down along their lines of descent through the generations of Man. They knew beyond all doubt, how vitally important it was, and still is for that matter, for human beings to establish and maintain contact with a higher Source of Consciousness which holds the only hopes available to humanity for ever becoming more than merely mortal and expendable entities of Earth alone. They had realised that contacts between humans and this "Ultramind" were very similar to sex-principles. One good germinal session lasting maybe only moments, began another chain of living consciousness which would go on growing and developing through an entire Life-cycle during which it was likely to germinate others of its own kind, or in some way influence the course of human affairs in its circle of activity. The Wise Ones were only trying to work out along spiritual lines the same Laws of Life applying in physical dimensions. Their experience taught them this was entirely practical.

For instance, they found it possible to make such "depth-contacts" best under conditions which could be arranged by their own efforts in co-operation with natural resources. A lot of their methods may seem crude or cruel to us, but we should remember they, like ourselves, had to use just what they could adapt in accordance with the identical intention which motivated them no less that it still moves us along the same Line of Life. Those old Wise ones knew that a single satisfactory union with Universal Awareness would result in a strangely altered awareness arising in them which might subsequently prove the salvation of their people in times of need at some future epoch. This is an interesting point. They did not expect "instant illumination" or any such impossibility. On initial impregnatory impact, such "God-germs" might even seem quite crazy or impossible. Initiated recipients made no more attempt to analyse or investigate these "Gifts" than a newly made mother normally tries to consider the character and life-history of her freshly entered embryo. They did just the same as a mother would—let the Light-Seed go naturally down inside themselves to its proper level, then allowed the Spirit of Life to germinate and grow this charge of consciousness as It would until the correct birthtime came in due Cosmic course.

We think so many modern ideas wonderful, but do we realise just how long ago they were planted in the far-off deep-down consciousness of perhaps only a very few humans who reached out for them towards the Great Lightgiver? How much do any of us realise our indebtedness to those in the past who gained the initial impregnations of intelligence which have only come to birth recently in our history? What was once conceived within the confines of these Old Stone Circles, which being much later born, has brought us to our present time? We can only fairly discharge our undoubted debt to our Lightleaders of the past, if we are prepared to make Inner contacts for ourselves now which will gestate through our collective consciousness until their birthtime comes at the correct season of the future. That is the message which the Rollrights and other Stone Circles will always hold for humanity. That was, and yet is, the ageless Fertility Faith on which they are founded. Those who think that principles of fertility are only concerned with physical sexual practices should widen their viewpoints. There is a more important spiritual side to this Inner issue, and that is the angle at which we are approaching the Rollrights now.

The Wise old ones of the Circle found out from both experience and Inner promptings, that if a number of procedures were carried out according to a prearranged pattern, a contact with the Intelligence they sought could almost be guaranteed. This brought spiritual events to some degree within their control, which was a great step along their Inner paths of progress. What they had done was calculate a set Pattern aimed at producing extended conditions of consciousness as an end effect. Otherwise, they had worked out a definite Ritual intended to result in realisations reaching beyond the ordinary limits of their average awareness. It was the reconstruction of this in suitable terms for our times which motivated many visits to the Stones under such varied conditions of season and circumstances.

There is not much mystery about the methods employed in olden times. Almost any psychologically instructed person might guess them now. They worked mostly by the stress-rest-stimulus system. Push endurance to a point where it seems to be cracking under the strain, then suddenly relax pressure into a state of most blessed relief. At the precise point where this becomes enjoyable, introduce some stimulus which captivates consciousness because of an intense interest aroused. Just as this is being followed along nicely, apply a fresh type of stress that demands attention elsewhere, and so on through a complete cycle of changes rising in higher and higher arcs until a peak plateau of Inner perceptivity is reached. This might almost be called the "Pain-Pleasure-Push-Perceive" cycle of consciousness. It can be very crude and cruel on lowest levels, but may perfectly well be modified and adapted in accordance with modern advances made after many sad centuries of spiritual experience.

To get some ideas of what such a Ritual was based on, and how it was most probably formed in the first place, it is necessary to have some appreciation of the ground-pattern covering the Rollright complex. There is not only a Circle, but also a megalith known as the King Stone, and what is presumed to be the remains of a dolmen now called the Whispering Knights. Originally there must have been other structures than these which fitted into the picture, and we shall have to find out how they were all put together in order to make good spiritual sense by the complete combination. Somehow they must tell a story which the old Wise ones would have understood in their time and tongue, we may grasp in ours now, and our remote descendants will be able to follow also. Let the Stones speak for themselves to start with.

CHAPTER FOUR

THE PATTERN OF THE PLACE

All the Rollrights show the world today is a skeleton. The reduced remnants of what they used to be. Once upon a time, the Circle was solid all the way round except for the rather narrow entrance formed by the overlapping of both ends so that no break could be seen from outside. An entrance of this sort could be guarded very easily or barricaded rapidly if urgently necessary. The Circle of major Stones representing all the families in the area which mattered, formed the anchors so to speak, and the interstices between them were filled up with piles of lesser, though still large rocks, signifying all the relatives and anticipated offspring connected with the principle pillars of the community. The total height of this enclosure was probably not more than about seven feet at most, but the effect was to provide privacy and some degree of seclusion for those occupying its interior.

Although a palisaded perimeter went around the Circle on its outside as well, the principal purpose of all this arrangement was security rather than impregnability. Though the confines of the Circle could most certainly be defended against small groups of marauders or a few unentitled intruders, it could not possibly have been held for any great time against a determined attack by superior numbers of invaders. The Circle builders obviously did not anticipate any such large scale raids against them. Their aim was to exclude minority intrusions rather than repel quantities of hostile humans. It was a case of safeguarding private property from depredations, for their fortifications would not have withstood anything of a really serious siege. The Stones were a guard against sneak-thieves, cattle-raiders, predators and other enemies of society who have always harassed human attempts to conduct affairs of life in a civilised manner. It might be said that the Circle was burglar proof rather than bomb proof. Not only was it a social centre, but also a commercial and trading stronghold in which valuables and commodities could be stored with relative safety.

We are apt to forget that people of those times travelled around somewhat more than might be supposed. Travel conditions may have been tough and formidable, but then, so were the people as well. They had to compete against the conditions of their period just as we do ours. By the time the Rollrights were set up, what we should call trading stations were established along many trade routes extending to the Western world. These became highly developed in the East long before the West became properly organised into the procedure. The principle was simple enough. Those with something to sell sought buyers, and so needed somewhere safe to effect such a transaction, which might take up several days hard bargaining. Therefore traders began to combine, and every important community set up what became a caravanserai, or security-station where merchants might meet, unload their goods, rest and recuperate, or otherwise operate their legitimate undertakings for the benefit of all in the vicinity and their own advantage.

In this way, commerce and civilisation went together. In the sign of the Circle they met and still remain. A Circle like the Rollrights had many facilities to offer. Sometimes, for instance, traders might wish to leave a store of goods in one place while they went elsewhere on some particular errand of enterprise. In the guarded safety of a Stone Circle, these stores were likely to be secure for at least a short while, and the traders found it profitable to pay the local authorities for this protection. To some extent, the Circle acted as banking houses do today, and stood security against anticipated profits. The Rollrights were certainly constructed by a prosperous and industrious people whose civil and commercial influence extended over the whole area and was most probably linked with lines of communication going much further than that, away in the wide world.

All this achievement did not happen overnight, however, and was only the end result of long and often bitter struggles for survival among much less circles of living. Fights, feuds, and factions went on all over the place among small groupings to an extent where everyone's existence became most uncertain. The causes of conflict then were just the same as now. Fear and greed; property and power. The old, old story. First of all humans had to unite against Nature in order to stay on this Earth, then they had to unite against each other in order to hold whatever piece of Nature their ancestors had managed to grab. What with constant struggles against the hazards of nature and fellow humans as well, life was getting very difficult for the nice simple souls of any age, who only ask to plod along peacefully and cultivate their particular patch with the general welfare of everyone at heart. So it seems still, for that matter.

Of course, these folk followed out customs handed down to them from Circle practices of primitive times, and still continued in community Circles everywhere. They stuck stone piles up at various points of territory they regarded as their particular province, and hoped outsiders would leave their herds and holdings alone. They might as well have relied on a modern politician's promise. Encroaching appropriations removed these landmarks with the speed of a demolition gang attacking a compulsory purchased property. Soon the sons of one family were slaughtering those of another, and Cain and Abel fought yet another round of their unfinished battle. Even the dimmest witted survivor could see that such a state of affairs was getting everyone nowhere that mattered very much.

Sooner or later an original pattern repeated itself again. Someone had to set up a Stone to end strife and establish a system of overlordship which would sort people out into communal categories and get them going round in relatively smooth circles again. This time no single leader was strong enough to do this all by himself, so a federation of force combined among the few families powerful enough to police the entire area and keep it in order for the sake of social survival. Especially the survival of those establishing their superiority in this way. These set up their special Stone not only to commemorate a victory of order over disorder, but also to point out the position of authority in that particular area, and the principles of rulership in general. This was, and still is, the King-Stone.

Apart from being a mere war memorial, that single Stone stood for one acknowledged Government presiding over the people who lived throughout the whole countryside around. It had a practical as well as symbolic significance, since it was the point from which all the various ownerships or minor sovereignties over visible land tracts could be determined. The King-Stone is a bulky affair which needed a good number of powerful men to put into place. Probably one member from each family around came to erect it. No small number of marker-movers could possibly sneak up and shift the King-Stone under cover of darkness. In any case, too many people knew exactly where it stood, so there would be no point in moving it, anyway.

Just how many leaders formed themselves into a "King-combination", and carved up the surrounding territory into definite individual areas of influence is very uncertain. The probability is about twelve. Of their number, one became selected as a "King of Kings" who eventually had to die as a kind of "purchase price" for the fidelity of the populace. The reason for this was based on very deep psychological principles indeed. In general the mass majority of mankind accepted the authority of powerful political and military governments just as they do today, but nevertheless they still felt fundamentally that something they needed was lacking. This factor, of course, was their freedom to become individual authorities on their own accounts, though they probably did not realise as much consciously. Inwardly they resented or resisted being brought under the control of a central "King-committee" which interfered so much with their natural liberties. There were many advantages to the system insofar as they were punitively prevented from feuds and free fights, and so could devote themselves to more prosperous pastimes. Moreover, the governing authorities had some ideas of organisation and discipline which they imposed on their people in terms of laws and conventions. The trouble was that these Kings diverted so much of everyone's efforts into their own personal accounts. The differential between what folk had for themselves and the Kings demanded as supershares of the communal capital was out of all fair proportion altogether. Even Stone Age peasantry realised and resented the imposition of a tax-burden they also knew to be a necessary evil of their growing social structure. So they naturally became restless, rebellious, and increasingly difficult to manage without a lot of repressive measures which only impaired their output abilities.

Once more, no one can be certain who first thought of "throwing one to the wolves" in order to appease not the anger of God, but of Man. The fact remains that if one of the Kings were periodically and ceremonially slain in the presence of all his people, this sacrifice had a profound effect upon their entire attitudes to life and their immediate environments. The sight of a Ruler being reduced to a mass of flesh and blood no different from anyone else's carved up carcase was a very sobering spectacle indeed. To see the highest and mightiest in the land solemnly brought down to the lowest common denominator of human existence on Earth—a butchered body—was an emotional and psyche-altering experience of the deepest significance. There was a communal feeling of emphatic equality with the new-killed King, which became superseded by a sense of surviving superiority. Especially if the ceremony was concluded by a shareout of the meat and drink provided by the flesh and blood of the martyred monarch. This made everyone feel "as good as he was", and satisfied their Inner cravings for conditions of Kingship, or the privileges and position attached to the office. For a short while, anyway, they felt as good as their Gods, and this made them much more amenable to the conditions they were expected to accept on Earth among Mankind—at least for the time being.

What made the whole business seem so absolutely convincing to everyone was the undeniable fact that the sacrificed King happened to be an entirely voluntary victim. It was an essential condition to his assumption of office. Once selected, the best of everything was his until the moment of his departure. Food, clothes, ornaments, women, whatever he wanted had to be provided for his enjoyment while his term of office lasted. Then, quite of his own will, he had to lay all these privileges together with his naked body stripped of everything upon the altar or Stone of sacrifice, and allow himself to be slain unflinchingly on behalf of the people. Witnesses of such an act could see for themselves that if anyone in such a high position was only too willing to relinquish the lot for the sake of achieving spiritual status, there must be a tremendous amount of truth in what the symbolic renunciation stood for. Besides, there is something very unpleasingly satisfactory to human nature in watching someone of socio-political importance brought down to common clay. "Now he is no better than we are" is maybe the most equalising feeling an underprivileged person may have. Parisians present at executions during the Terror must have felt quite surfeited with social satisfaction.

Sacrificial Kings were not really difficult to find. Nor would they be today if a demand existed. Suppose some authority offered a million or upwards of pounds plus every gratification asked for during a year, in return for someone's public service of a comparatively painless death in dramatic circumstances, with a world-wide TV coverage? The selection committee would practically be killed themselves in the rush of applicants. No one knowing human nature need doubt this in the least. In olden days the incentives seemed even larger than that. Death was a commonplace incident, anyway, and a big enough bribe usually buys any sort of human offering in the end. For the sake of being considered a King for even a short time, many would gladly go to their deaths in that guise. So would it be in our day if occasion arose.

So, by the official sacrifice of occasional Kings, old time civil constitutions were kept together in their Circles under the control of a central government who knew how to handle the rank and file of massed humanity around it. Just how often such Kings were sacrificed is not clear. At first, fairly frequently it seems, probably several a year depending on local circumstances and exigencies. Then the occasions were soon cut to two a year, Summer and Winter, reducing to an annual event, and then a seven year celebration. It was not long before the Kings were offering substitutes instead of themselves, followed by animals instead of humans, then eventually vegetable products were substituted again in the shape of bread and wine as they still stand today. No matter how the King may be killed in one form, he always resurrects in another.

Methods of killing the King varied somewhat among different communities, but he was usually granted a quick and expert end. Sometimes his body was cooked and shared out as a sacred meal, but often his flesh was eaten raw in small morsels, his blood being drunk by the chosen few, and the remainder sprinkled over the assembly as a token of a spirit shared among everyone. Apparently at the Rollrights, Kings were sacrificed far less frequently than elsewhere, but when one had to die, he was stood before the King-Stone with his arms spread apart something like a crucified man, then was swiftly speared from the front up into the rib-cage straight to the heart. He was supposed to die in the sight of all the people, and before "both Eyes of Heaven". That meant just after sunrise at a full moon when the orbs of both luminaries came level. The death by spear is interesting, for, in the Grail Legend, it is always the Lance which appears as a Hallow dripping blood into the Cup. The connection of a spear with the conventional Crucifixion should also be noted.

The King's death had the effect of releasing many tribal tensions that had led to civil disturbances and private murders. It also enabled the people to feel part and parcel of the living community which kept such a sacrificial cycle going. Altogether, it was a central and culminating item in what would now be called a "public relations programme". When it was instituted, it might have been a measure of expediency for keeping people happy through a tension-target cum scape-goat sacrifice, but it was and still is based much further back upon spiritual principles of far deeper origin.

Fundamentally, the Sacred King principle ties up with the inherent Life-right of all humans to eventually become individual rulers over their own self-kingdoms, deciding whatever destiny for themselves they will by means of the Divine Intention within them. This basic factor of our spiritual genetics derives from our most distant origins reputed to have reached Earth from a very remote Cosmic source. Physically, it might be considered as the blood-link between humanity on Earth and the "early Kings" from elsewhere, who were the "sons of Gods" who fertilised the "daughters of Men". At all events, it amounts to Man's ineradicable instinct that somewhere back in himself lies a connection with Divinity Itself, and even the meanest human has a chance of attaining such a self-status if only this touch of the "Blood-Royal" can reach such a one and be developed to its full potential from one life to another.

It was generally recognised well enough that no ordinary mortal could possibly achieve this spiritual state during one incarnation alone. An unguessable number of human lives might be necessary, but the vital factor was to die in such a way that even a slightly closer contact with this "Blood-Royal" connection with Cosmos might be managed. A continued chain of advancing rebirths should result in any human soul becoming steadily higher and more individualistic in both a social and spiritual sense. So was the "Holy Grail" to be gained, and such still is its Mystery. One way or another, humans will always recognise this deeply in themselves, however dimly and distortedly it might reflect from their surface appearances.

So in the ritual drama of the Sacrificed King, early Man saw himself magnified and Deified according to the sacred hope held wordlessly within his most secret heart. With a visual, practical, and actually shared experience of this spiritual certainty, even the most harassed human could struggle along with Earthlife for a little while longer. Assured of ultimate Divinity at the end of an indefinite Life-line, the worst of Earth's adventures might be surmounted successfully. We should do well in our days to remember what has brought us this far along our time-track in search of Truth, and how much we still need the same stimulus to take us the remainder of our journey.

At the Rollrights, the Stone which stood for this King-sized Mystery of Mankind served as a pledge-point where men met and swore peace between each other. Once a hand had been placed on that Stone, and an intention of peace proclaimed, the penalty for breaking such a promise was an ignominious death. It was the only way to keep the land and its people more or less free from serious strife so that more prosperous pursuits than warfare could be followed. Somehow, this still seems to have a message worth hearing at present. Far from being silent, the Stones are yet speaking with very clear voices which tell of matters we need to know in our times maybe more than theirs. What they have to say is perhaps of greater importance now than when they first spoke of it several thousands years ago.

The power which people recognised at the King-Stone was mainly political and temporal, despite the spiritual substrata of such supreme importance. Yet there was an especially spiritual side provided in the pattern of the place. This was associated with the Whispering Knights or Counsellors. By the time the Rollrights were established in full working order, distinctions were gradually being discerned between the operations of "Church" and "State" as functional facets of human behaviour. Not that any sharp division existed between them, for they were regarded as just varied methods of doing the same thing. They did not seem to have separate hierarchies, and we might not even suspect now that any form of a definite Church existed then. It was far more as we might imagine some elementary sort of spiritualism or "inspirational activity." The actual way it was presented to the people was certainly fascinating, if the Stones are to be believed, and a mental reconstruction of the event is most intriguing.

When in new condition, the Counsellor Stones formed the central chamber of quite a sizable pyriform structure, mostly composed of smaller stones and turfs laid like bricks. There was a way into this chamber along a narrow little tunnel just big enough for a smallish person to crawl through. At the top, under the capstone, was a small ventilating shaft communicating with the outer air. This, in effect, was the Holy of Holies where the tribal Deity manifested a presence to mortals.

The secret was probably rather an open one. What actually happened on specially sacred occasions was that a human medium, generally an elderly female, would be sent inside the chamber where she went into a semi-trance condition, and called out whatever came to her inspirationally. Heard at a little distance outside, this would sound almost superhuman, and be taken as the direct voice of Divinity speaking to those assembled in anticipation of answers to their problems. An Oracle, in fact. We still employ them. How good the old ladies of the Rollrights were in comparison with ours, we shall never know. What we guess might make us sympathetic to the seekers in the past. Or maybe envious of them.

It seems that if the inside of the pyramid was warmed up previously by a turf fire for a day or so, the heat and smoke-smell greatly encouraged the wise woman or shamaness to "go off" into volubility for quite a while before she passed out into unconsciousness or even death. Not that her death was an actual objective as in the case of the King, but an incidental to be expected if the God so intended. When such a demise occurred, which was not a terribly rare event, the body was given honourable burial, and later the bones were lifted, cleaned, and put with others of the same class usually in a skin bag kept in a side-cyst of the main pyramid. In that way, the spirits of the ancestors were supposed to keep in touch with their living descendants. It was probably a commencement of the custom of storing saintly bones in sacred shrines.

We might watch from this distance of time one such female elder going into the warm darkness of her artificial cave. She is skin clad, and carries a skull rattle in addition to an amulet necklace clashing round her thin torso. She seems so small, ill-nourished, and frail, until we notice how sinewy and tough her stringy muscles are. Her age is difficult to estimate, though she looks incredibly ancient with her white hair bound back and her almost toothless gums receding in a hollowed and wind-wrinkled face. Yet her eyes seem bright and almost supernaturally sharp, though their focus is obviously not with this world any longer. She has the strangest sort of smile as she sinks to her knees before the short tunnel entrance and begins her crawl into the interior. Who does she expect to meet there? Only she will ever know, and it is certain she will never tell. Shall we ever see her alive again? If not, we know she has met death with the same willing confidence evinced by the King. Both King and Crone are part of the Pattern we are only beginning to understand in perchance the slightest degree.

From the front of the structure we shall take our places among a small crowd of people at a respectful distance facing the sort of forecourt marked out with small stones and staves. In this little area burns a fire which flickers and sends up smoke columns suggestive of spirits likely to appear at any moment. Tending the fire is another decorated devotee of the Deity whose task it is to select questions from the supplicants, ask these of the Oracle, then translate whatever answers are obtained in terms the recipient might just misunderstand enough to be fortunate with if any action were taken upon the advice. This exterior interpreter is usually male, and certainly has a well developed sense of showmanship, plus a shrewd insight into average human affairs.

The evening's entertainment begins as all shows do—with a curtain raising overture by the performer at the proscenium. He is a most versatile character. He drums, dances, chants, and goes through all sorts of antics. At first, he catches the attention of the audience by amusing them, but gradually leads them very skilfully into ever deeper and more serious channels, until they are hanging on every word and straining to follow his meanings, which grow more and more mysterious. The atmosphere becomes tense as he invokes the Voice of God from the interior of the silent and significant pile before them. Standing with upraised arms and uplifted voice, this fur draped figure would impress an audience of any era who saw him silhouetted against the firelight and smoke, or heard his impassioned pleas in their names for a direct answer from Divinity to their problems. He uses all possible persuasion, explaining to whatever Deity listened from the point of this pyramid exactly what was wanted or hoped for. He cajoled, reminded, begged, hinted, and sometimes suggested just what Mankind, and these people in particular demanded of Divinity in exchange for their allegiance. With all the skill at his command, he put the case for the present assembly fairly and squarely before Whoever might be willing to hear from this holy height ahead. When both he and his audience felt sufficient had been said or shouted, he fell suddenly silent, and everyone held themselves still and quiet, scarce daring to breathe for fear of blowing away the spirit they felt was coming among them.

Out of the silence at last came the smallest of sounds. Only the sensitive ears of those old timers could pick it up at first. It was actually the medium in her cave-chamber keening quietly to herself and rattling away with her skull and knuckle bone contrivance. To those outside, now led and suggestively controlled by their priestly president, it must have sounded like a direct reply from the Almighty. Louder and shriller came the uncanny cry from the cavernous echo chamber of the Counselling Stones until it stopped, leaving a dramatic silence. The old woman was trying to get her breath back, though none outside heard her wheezes. Her external partner announced with suitable sibilance that some God was at last present. The people scarcely needed telling. They might feel as much for themselves. Appropriately awestruck, they waited for whatever celestial communication might follow.

In their name, the priest asked the Presence what was in everyone's mind. Who had come to them in spirit shape? How were they to know the identity of the intelligence addressing them? Quite often, the answer was guessed in advance, but this time they had a seldom known surprise. Those close enough heard clearly uttered the name of the King they had seen sacrificed with their own eyes that very morning. He had returned to them in person as a God-spirit and was speaking to them from the Other World at that very instant. From this vantage point he would listen to their petitions, give them good advice, and remove many responsibilities of life from their already burdened shoulders. He still cared enough about his people to come back from the dead on their account. Where he had gone, the rest might follow in due course. It was all very wonderful and the people felt both flattered and gratified that such a mighty personage was able to intervene on their behalf with the Powers making human wishes possible. There, right before them, was proof positive of how life had to triumph over death in the end. The King was dead, long live the King. May he live forever indeed.

Acting on behalf of the people, the priest now put their questions to the invisible influence presumed present. It might be supposed all sorts of important theological issues and mystical matters might be raised. Did anyone ask what it felt like to die and return again? Did someone even thank the deceased for taking so much trouble on everyone's account? Was anything of mystical significance enquired upon? Who evinced any particular interest in spiritual subjects? Regrettably not a single person showed the slightest interest or sign of concern with such momentous matters. They were all so engrossed with their everyday and ordinary affairs that these were the only topics on which they sought guidance or appealed for favours. However impressed they might be by Heavenly demonstrations, their main motives for dealing with these were the Earthly advantages they hoped to gain if the Hidden Powers might be persuaded to grant them. They were a sadly materialistic crowd, and they more or less got the kind of answers they deserved. Ambiguous and ambivalent, all full of ifs and buts, possible to interpret whichever way events went. If they were dissatisfied with these, no one seemed to show it very much. Who were they to argue with a God? At any rate, they went away afterwards back to the Circle in a firmer frame of mind than before. They evidently got something out of the experience that did them some good.

An interesting feature of this event was that the presence of the old woman in the pyramid was no particular secret from the people as a whole. Doubtless there were those somewhat too dim to connect her with the strange voices and incoherent gabble they heard issuing from the top of the pyramid. The whole production depended on what is now called "suspension of disbelief", or the deliberate acceptance of appearances for the sake of following out a presented story. This happens all the time people watch a stage, screen, or a TV show. They know well enough that a TV set is only a box full of electronic equipment, but they are still prepared to react with the pictures it shows them in order to enjoy emotional or intellectual experiences. They are not so much intentionally deceiving themselves, as voluntary opening up their awareness to Inner dimensional actualities represented by symbolic occurrences portrayed with human actors.

It would be so easy to dismiss the whole of this episode as a dirty piece of sheer deception or a pious and pompous fraud. We could match it in our days with a thousand similar incidents. On the surface it would seem to condemn the fundamental of religious faith in general as nothing but wishful thinking and a good deal of delusion mixed up with self-aggrandising fantasy. Something of that nature anyway. This solution seems so obvious that there has to be a far deeper meaning concealed somewhere underneath it. Why would humans of any era act in such a way to begin with? What possible reason makes them suppose for one instant that anybody might survive the destruction of a physical corpus? All their evidence points to the contrary. They have eaten the human remains of the departed among them. If this does not certify his death, nothing will. True, they have heard voices or rumours of voices claiming to be connected with the late regent, but if their ears are ready to believe one thing, their stomachs expect them to affirm precisely the opposite. Just what makes them so anxious to suspend their disbeliefs in favour of such an unlikely aftermath? Entirely apart from the authenticity or otherwise of the ritual drama they participated in, why were, and still are, people willing to accept that particular pattern of symbolism? Presented in antithesis, they would reject it entirely. What is spiritually special about this faith-formula?

Man is so made that he must instinctively try and live according to his inbuilt genetics both physically and also metaphysically. Intellect, reason, logic, and other artificial arrangements of our awareness may not conform in the least with the secret springs of consciousness arising from the very basics of our beings. No matter what our highly trained areas of awareness tell the formal focus of our ordinary mentalities, if this information opposes our deep-down basic beliefs of Life, then the resulting dissension throughout our Inner anatomies causes us very considerable trouble indeed. Most mental, spiritual, and physical sickness or disturbances comes from this very remote root. So do the majority of our social ills and unbalances. For Man to deny the Divinity which is basic to his being is the surest way to eventual disaster of some serious extent. This does, of course, depend on a definition of Divinity as the Life-Spirit of All comprising the individual entity of each.

Despite every evidence of death, Man knows without being told that he belongs to Life. Whatever happens to his body, the mind that moved it, or anything else to do with it, Man senses his survival through whatever states of existence may be needed to continue his course of living. There is no use asking anyone to prove this point or discuss the hows, whys and wherefores of it. Our human language does not go so far, but our recognition of wordless symbols will. That is why we accept their representations which we encounter on Earth. Those symbols speak in terms we can only interpret on the very Inmost levels of our living. There we come in contact with the Universal Consciousness in which our actual entities exist independently of incarnation or other forms of focal egoic expression.

So with the old time people who went through the "death and resurrection" drama of Life, and their modern inheritors of the same Tradition. It is the symbolic principles of the Life-laws which were and are so strongly recognised, rather than the actual practice presented to them. Even had the old woman, her priest partner, and whatever they said or did been entirely fraudulent as an act, the symbology of the proceedings would still have revealed truth to those requesting it with a profound purpose. It should be clearly understood that no lie can possibly be told unless there is a truth behind it to be misrepresented. This ought to be remembered in all our dealing with ritual procedures. Whatever we see that looks faked or phony should automatically send us inside ourselves looking for the truth it distorts.

Nor have we any real right to assume the entire events enacted around the prophetic pyramid were absolutely and utterly untrue. Human consciousness extended by stress or other pressures has an ability of making contact with far wider and different areas of awareness. Though the accuracy of communications established through these methods can scarcely be guaranteed, they have definitely been known to produce occasionally remarkable results. There is no doubt that the pythoness and her partner cheated consciously or subconsciously just as much as modern mediums have, and probably from the same motives, but nevertheless, we have no reason for supposing it was all false and futile. Certainly something "came through". Something which helped people to live and afforded them enough inspiration for lifting themselves even a little up the scale of evolution. However phony the priest-pythoness combination may have meant to be, there were times when they felt themselves "taken over" by a far greater consciousness than theirs over which they had no control at all. The Spirit of Life does indeed blow where It will now and again among Mankind. Besides, there were many occasions when perfectly sound and sincere souls officiated. The messages they obtained for sincere seekers from Inner sources must have caused chains of circumstances reaching right down to our present times. Who knows how far one good word will go until it is uttered?

It seems that after the ceremonies of the Counsellors, people went back to the Circle and celebrated their companionship with one another as humans do when they are pleased with each other's persons. They ate, drank, sang, danced, and enjoyed all the amenities available. If time-travellers of today were transported back there in high hopes of witnessing wonderful sexual orgies, they would be most sadly disappointed. What coupling did take place, was conducted with surprising reticence. Worse scenes can be viewed in public parks today. In Circle-times, couples went off by themselves away from the crowd and performed in private. They may have run a barrage of ribald remarks sometimes, though this was not a usual custom at all. Moreover, fairly strict taboos on unsuitable mating were coming into force at that period, and disobedience to established rulings meant a dishonourable death. On the whole, there was less sexual laxity then than now, despite the difference in codes and customs.

During these social Circle-gatherings, members mostly grouped up close to their family Stones and tended to remain in loose association with them throughout the proceedings. They felt vaguely that this enabled the spirits of their ancestors to share the enjoyment with them. Oldsters were apt to stay close to the Stones while middle-aged people mingled more widely, and the youngsters tore around the place until firmly directed otherwise by elders. One of the first things any tribal child had to learn was how to find its own proper family Stone in the Circle and stay with it if ordered. The rough and ready method was to march the child up to the Stone, make him examine it closely while the family call or recognition signal was given in his ear, then he was taken to another part of the Circle and spun round in order to bemuse him. On a word of command he had to locate his Stone immediately among all the others and run instantly to it, there remaining in an attitude of alertness. Failure to do this promptly enough resulted in a sharp slap or so. Most lads learned rapidly how to recognise their Stones and come to them when called. The reason for all this was to ensure a satisfactory response at times of emergency, and also to instil a sense of Tradition into young people whose birthrights were bound up with fellow tribal members. This custom has survived today in rather a mutilated condition as the practice of "beating the bounds" in a parish or district in order to show youngsters their places in relation to the remainder of the local population.

So far, three distinct items of the Rollright complex have been considered. The King-Stone, the Counsellors, and the Circle. Each had its especial function and proper place in the complete Pattern, but something seemed definitely lacking which ought to have been there, yet not a trace of it remained. This deficiency nagged like a missing tooth for quite a while until it was quietly supplied through Inner information and subsequently located on last century archaeological drawings depicting a crude arrangement of small stones now removed altogether, since they seemed of no particular significance. They were actually a sort of "Gatehouse" to the whole area, insofar as they served as a shelter for whatever civil official was on duty whose job it was to receive and dispatch visitants and departures to and from the whole place. However we think of this in comparison with our modern Customs, Immigration Office, or whatever else, this facility was the proper entry and departure point for the civic centre of the locality.

It was not much to look at as an erection. Little more than a thatch supported on corner poles covering a smallish stone walled enclosure. In this, a number of men were normally kept in readiness for emergencies and necessary communal services. Not a large number—possibly some twenty or so, if that. There were runners for sending on messages. A few tough types well armed for police work. An officer with a variety of duties from interrogating and dealing with newcomers, to making sure that those quitting the community were not leaving undue debts behind them or unsettled quarrels of a serious nature. To this point agents from other areas first reported, enquiries were made, and initial contacts established with the community. It was a most useful institution altogether, though there is no purpose in pretending it was run as well as modern places of its kind, or organised to any equivalent extent.

One custom which seemed to be imposed upon visitants and those passing through the Rollright complex was a kind of toll, tax, or hostage demanded from them at this particular point. This could be any token they bore on their persons such as an ornament of value, fur garment, or maybe a piece of merchandise they had with them. It might be an animal or a child. There were two main reasons for this. First, it was some guarantee of good behaviour on the visitors' parts, since some of the surrendered items were returned to them on departure, and secondly, the local authorities divided the rest among them. In addition, it was a sort of check on foreigners. One look at the heap of tokens in the guardhouse would give a good idea of aliens present. The system was very far from infallible, but at least it attempted something which today controls the comings and goings of people round a whole world. We need not speculate on its failures, breakdowns, bribery, and similar human blunderings. The thing to remember is that this was a conscious attempt at controlling or regulating the flow of humanity through and around their chosen course of life.

Here pledges were made which amounted to acknowledgements of local laws and customs which visitors were expected to observe while in the area. We do as much with passport visas today. In effect, the rules of the place were read and respected. Only those likely to obey them and behave properly were supposed to be admitted to the Circle, but of course this could never be enforced entirely. It did prevent some unknown undesirables from inflicting themselves unduly on the community, however. The overall idea was to encourage types of visitors with anything of value in the way of skills, abilities, or actual trade goods to offer, and deter or eject those who only came to steal, cheat, or otherwise impose upon the rightful inhabitants of this civilised state. Of course this was impractical. Most good ideas are, but we may achieve something like it if we persist long enough. There seems no reason why we should abandon hope after only a few millennia have passed.

This brings us up to four distinct functional points of what we may call the Rollright Plan, out of which we should be able to construct a reliable Ritual for relating ourselves with the Life-Principles they still stand for. It would only be stupid to propose that precisely the same things should be done nowadays which were put into practise then, and yet there has to be a linkage between customs connected through the centuries. The solution of this problem lies with finding satisfactory symbolism to contain and conjoin the concepts of consciousness concerned into an harmonious and acceptable whole. Once more we must go in and behind the Stones on deeper levels still.

CHAPTER FIVE

THE RULES OF THE RITE

There was no hint whatever in expecting the original builders of the Rollrights to explain or expound the mystical principles underlying their ritualised procedures. They were not consciously aware of these themselves, and so could leave no recorded impression in the Stones they left behind them. Nevertheless, the clues of consciousness they had imparted to their memorials did eventually lead deeply enough for contact to be made with an entirely different type of intelligence which appeared willing to communicate symbolically the sense of what lay back of that which had already been gathered. Beyond an acknowledgement of indebtedness to this source of Inner information there is no call to identify it more closely here.

To start with, it was necessary to consider the layout or "fundamental formula" for the Rollright complex. There were four definite structures calling for attention. Suppose these were placed in "light-order", or according to the circuit of Cosmos we call "clockwise" or deosil, how would that work out? Going round them in turn, there was first the "Gate", then the King-Stone, then the Counsellors, and lastly the Circle. Or was the Circle last? Might it be possible to go out of the complex again by the same or another door as in we went? If so, that might explain quite a good deal. What if we took these four Stations and equated them with the Four Magical Concepts of Cosmos? Could such a connection be established? Providing this were possible, appropriate rituals would almost fall into place round a framework specifically arranged for that very purpose. Suppose each of the four Rollright Stations were summed up and given an adequate cover code-name? Would that help? It did.

"Gateway" was both an In and an Out. The In of our lives is via a Womb, and the Out through a Tomb. Therefore, if this point were termed the Tomb-Womb, or vice versa, depending which way one faced the course of Cosmos, that would cover both the entrance and exit of this experience. A Womb-Tomb symbol is like a Door between Inner and Outer Life. It all depends which side we knock on. In our excarnate condition we need to enter a human Womb in order to live on Earth. When we come to the end of Earthlife, we have to enter some sort of Tomb which becomes the Womb for our emergence into another Lifestate. Back and forth we travel in search of Truth until we earn exemption by means of nullifying the necessity.

The Magical Symbol here is the Sword. It signifies a "cutting off" and a "point of penetration" among other meanings. In one way it might bring death, and in another, deliverance from death. It has two edges but only one point. Most importantly it represents the "Sword-Bridge" crossing of the Chasm between Life and Death. If a Sword is stabbed downward into an open tomb, this symbolises either a death-stroke or a phallic life-thrust into a Womb. A double meaning all round. Assuming that we are facing toward our death-point and about to enter another condition of living beyond that limit, the Sword is certainly the correct Symbol to employ in such an instance.

It is granted that the original Rollrighters did not have swords, but slew with spears. In their time the equivalent of our Sword would be an arrow or a throwing flint. Nor was this their sacrificial stage. We are simply starting with the fundamentals of a Life-pattern, and beginning each cycle of change between Inner and outer existence by a representation of a Birth or Death act depending on which direction we intend taking. In any case, it is really the same act inversed. Here, we shall still assume we are leaving Earth life behind and continuing our course of consciousness around the Great Circuit that eventually brings us back to birth again. Our Inner wanderings presently bring us up against a spiritual solidity symbolised by the King-Stone, and simply called here the Stone.

This amounts to the weight of karmic burdens we carry with us, signifies the sacrifices we shall have to make in order to equalise them, and mainly points out the code of conduct we should uphold as the spiritual standard which ought to govern our behaviour like a King rules his people. It generally corresponds with the Judgment we have to make upon ourselves when we come to view our lives with Inner eyes opened after our physical eyes have finally closed. The Stone stands for recognition of Lifelaws and appreciation of a necessity to observe them scrupulously. Above all it speaks of a Kingdom which exists for everyone able to rise in themselves to such an exalted rank. To claim this, it is necessary to establish kinship with the Blood-Royal, as will be indicated later on.

The Magical Symbol here is the Rod or Staff. This is "the measure of a man", or the rule by which a rightful King persuades his people to live properly. In each individual case, the Rod means the central guide line we should apply to ourselves if we are to stand like the Stone firmly and steadfastly upright between Heaven (the sky) and Earth (the ground). It also signifies the support we may rely on from our firmly founded faith, which will both point our way ahead and help us travel toward our objectives. In the case of the old time Sacred Kings who were once slain here, it was the Rod in the form of a spear or lance which sent them off on their "Sky journey". It was not considered that the spear killed them on that occasion. Instead, it liberated their spirits, thus bringing life and not death. No one spoke of the King after his send-off as if he were dead in the sense of being non-existent. He had changed his life-condition for a still higher one. He lived, not died, but he had earned this immortality by his conduct and the manner of his going. He had given an example in the eyes of everyone how a Man should live in order to leave a body behind and become "as the Gods—immortal." His Symbol was the Staff-sceptre of the Rod, and the Spear-Lance of liberation. We may see it now in the upright of the Calvary Cross. The transverse arm is the beam of that Balance by which all are judged and weighed up for what they are spiritually worth to Life.

All this and much more derives from the symbology of the Rod to be encountered in company with the Stone, yet there is infinitely more still to be met with in the course of Earthlife or its Afterlife. Immortality may be a difficult condition to achieve, but it is much harder to experience. Imagine an ordinary life without the solace of sleep. Then imagine an Afterlife without the relief of unbeing. All Inner Traditions agree that if the Supreme Spirit of Life ceased consciousness for the slightest instant, the whole of Creation and every individual therein would also end entirely at the same moment. To intend immortality as a self-state is a supreme responsibility which only the bravest souls are likely to accept. No wonder that "Faithful King" was such an honoured title for human concepts of Divinity. Having achieved a symbolic semblance of this state with the Stone of Kings—where next? What is greater than Kingship? There is an answer. Kind kinship. Love in the true sense of the term. Union with the Life-Spirit on deepest levels resulting in a real relationship with all that lives. Not a mere "brotherhood of Man", but a blood-brotherhood with all Being Itself.

The communication of the Life-Mystery comes through "dwelling in illuminated darkness" surrounded by the protection of Perfect Peace. This overall description of the circumstances covered by the Counsellors of the Rollrights may be coded as "The Cave". Here is the deepest state of spiritual stillness in which every single self must meet the Divinity Within. To be alone yet accompanied by all. To be in darkness yet illuminated to the utmost. To have died, yet continue living eternally. To be unconscious of anything, yet Aware as everything. The contradictions that contain

Cosmos. All these profound points and their associative realisations are connected with the Cave concept presented by the Counsellors.

A Cave almost immediately suggests the Mithraic and Christian Mysteries. It brings us the origin and end of Life where the "Blood of Life" in the form of Light begins and ceases. In some rare presentations of the Rollright Mystery Drama, the Sacred King was not killed outright at the Stone, but severely wounded in the groin. The now Lamed King had to hobble or drag himself to the Cave, leaving a trail of blood all the way. Then he crawled into the Cave to die alone in the darkness of its sanctuary. This was the most heroic death of all in the eyes of those who acclaimed it. The blood of the King brought Life to Earth and the people thereof, while the King himself ascended to Heaven by the Holy Mountain. From thence, his blood would descend again in the form of Fire (sunshine) and Water (rain) for the prosperity of all people. The legend is eternal, and accompanies Life from one end to the other.

What other Magical Symbol for the Cave could there be except the Cup? It bears the Blood, and if filled with oil instead becomes a lamp of Light. In old days the sacred Cup was commonly made from the skull of a sacrificial King. So it might be the vessel bearing the blessed Blood of immortality among those chosen to share this privilege, or else a source of Light illuminating them with Infinite Wisdom. In either case, it conveys the same message. Light and Life are interchangeable energies.

One use for the Cave in early days was an initiatory ordeal-chamber. Candidates were put inside to survive with themselves alone in the darkness for a whole night and even longer. All they could feel were the skeletons of those bony brethren who silently shared their constriction, and all they smelt was death. Either they conquered their terrors and learned the "secret word" which would ensure their release at daybreak, or they went insane and were left to die in disgrace. Brutal maybe, but so was Life sometimes. Besides, those candidates were entirely volunteers like the King. Eventually arrangements were made so that the light of dawn came through a small ventilating crevice under the capstone which the occupant did not know about, and illuminated a symbol painted on the stone surface opposite. If the initiate were sane and sensible enough to interpret this glyph or say the right words about it, those hearing his voice outside proclaimed him a worthy member of the Mystery, and rolled away the Stone which blocked the entrance. Then all together shared the Cup of Light which had been well and truly earned. What more dreadful ordeal can any living person endure than to be cast into their own depths of darkness in self-solitude and there face the Truth Within?

The only hope of surviving this spiritual state of ultimate stress lies with the contents of Cup symbolising a capacity for living consciousness. This comes from the line of blood or breeding behind humans, and also from the contents of their "cranium cups", which they should have filled by their efforts at understanding the essentials of Life. Put bluntly, someone of good breeding and adequate education ought to survive and transcend the worst trials of existence far better than less matured mortals. To belong with the right "Blood-line" reaching back to Divine ancestry was and yet is, the prerogative of whoso passes this point of peril properly.

The Cup not only holds Life and Light. It offers Love, or co-union with Cosmos. "Being of one Blood" unites all that lives into a single and eternal Family. In a very minor and microcosmic manner, celebrants with the symbolic Cup bound themselves into a "faith-family" whose aim it was (and still should be) to live in love with each other forever. It is the maximum that Mankind may ever expect to attain and still remain Man in his highest spiritual state. That is the deep significance of the Cup communion here. After that, we are absorbed into the Absolute and achieve Perfect Peace Profound, or else re-continue our cycle of Cosmos on our way back to incarnatory living. This time, however, we shall return with the blessing of what we have become by our Cup-contact. Others may share this through our increased abilities and more advanced capabilities of consciousness which will accompany us from henceforth as we plod around the Pathway of Life we select for ourselves. On each incarnatory round, we ought to bring with us just that extra and vital impact of Life on highest levels which leads us ever up the Cosmic climb of evolution. So shall we ultimately enter that Light which none leave evermore.

If we are to return into incarnation, we cannot very well remain in constant communion with Life through the Cup. So we shall continue around the course until we arrive at the Circle which is otherwise called "The Field". It is a Field in all senses of the word. A field of fertility, a field of force, a field of action. We might equate it with the Elysian Fields here, or the Inner area where consciousness is cultivated, promoted, and propagated in order to produce the finest crop of individual and intelligent characters that Creation can raise.

Until now round the circuit it has been very much of an exclusive process, each soul making its own direct relationship with the principle behind all points. Here all individuals are brought together on more or less equal terms to sort out their various categories of living and arrange particulars of mutual association with each other. People have to learn how to live with other people for what they are in and as themselves. This is the area where folk should be able to acquire such an invaluable art in ideal conditions of consciousness. Some call it "Heaven", but it amounts to a state of society in which every single life sustains a wholly harmonious and happy relationship with all the rest while simultaneously remaining a self-determining entity in its own right. An unachieved state of Life on this Earth as yet, but still an inspiration and spiritual suggestion which helps us face an uncertain future.

The layout of the Field shows that harmonious happiness among any number of humans or other life-types depends upon everyone being correctly related with the rest according to the true nature of the Life-pattern basic to himself and all others. All should be as they will because they belong precisely with their particular points in that especial spiritual structure of Life. It is almost as if a Plan of Perfection already existed in the Universal Awareness, and all living beings were allotted their own unique point in this picture, but had to achieve such a position by their own wills entirely. Only when and if everyone is absolutely self-satisfied in a spiritual sense not only with his own life, but with all other lives around him, could a state of "Heaven" be assumed in actuality. We are certainly not likely to encounter it on Earth as yet, but as an ideal it may help us out of hell somewhat sooner.

This "Heavenstate" is where people can really enjoy each other's company and at the same time sort themselves out into suitable categories for further incarnations. Here are the basic genetic blocks or Stones from which all the different races, nations, and family connections spring. All have their proper place within this Circle, but that does not mean a change agreeable to all concerned is impossible if opportunity allows. The trouble is that most souls have to squeeze in wherever they can, or otherwise take what comes instead of awaiting exactly the right Cosmic circumstances to suit their special spiritual characteristics. Theoretically, it should be possible to find one's Cosmically correct Life-incidence in this Circle, and follow on from that point in a state of Inner harmony or "Heaven" wherever an individual course may lead. It is a question of finding the "Family" where one rightly belongs by links of "The Blood", and relating with the remainder of Life through those channels of consciousness.

The Magical Symbol here is naturally the Shield. This in itself is a "field" upon which is emblazoned a combination of characters called a "charge". The function of a Shield is not only to protect someone's integrity, but also proclaim the pattern making that individual exactly what he is or hopes to be. We need both these facilities while trying to live anywhere, "Heaven" not excepted. Firstly, we should have a state of security unassailable by others of our kind. Then we ought to have clear-cut and concise conceptions of what we are, will be, and how we mean to become whatever we intend. The substance and shape of the Shield provides the first requirement, and its charge or motto outlines the second.

A Shield is not intended to be an aggressive, but a defensive, instrument. It is for preserving peace more than making war with. We do not only shield ourselves from other people, but we ought equally to shield them from our own injurious influences. Every time we intervene between our instincts or abilities to injure and likely recipient of this ill-will, a Magical or spiritual Shield has been properly used. In this way, harmony is preserved all round the Circle. We definitely need our Shields in this world, and evidently there is a place for their Inner equivalents in the Other-state. "Heaven" is always taken to be a Cosmic condition in which those rightfully there are automatically shielded from all which would be inimical to their happiness. Even in this world we pray for the "protection of Providence" or otherwise to be shielded from destructive dangers. Given adequate shielding, we can survive the worst our world may threaten us with, but without such protection scarcely a step can be taken securely.

The design or "charge" on a Magical Shield should show how to live so that a whole-hearted and healthy state of spiritual security becomes perfectly possible. Each entity has its own inherent ideas about achieving this happy condition of Life, and so arrives at the "Magical Motto" or Key-code around which its Inner living is arranged. That is why so much importance was attached to the conscious adoption of a symbolic equivalent by members of "Magical" Orders. In the context of the Rollright experience here, it signifies entering the Circle in company with kindred souls, then arriving at an understanding of what Life is all about as a self-relationship with Divinity and Humanity alike. This accomplished, the realisation has to be coded up into consciousness and emblazoned on the individuality as a self-Shield which will take the bearer anywhere and everywhere through Life according to need of its experience.

Equipped with a satisfactory Shield and regenerated by the refreshing remembrance of Elysian encounters, a Life-emergent entity should be ready to tackle another incarnation in the best of spirits. How to return? Through the other side of the Doorway. The same Gate which had "Tomb" inscribed on it as we came into this complex, has "Womb" imprinted on its inner surface. It is just a question of which way we point ourselves.

Earth is the mouth which eats up our deceased bodies, but she is also the Mother who offers us a new one in exchange. This time we need not fear to face her any more than previously. Both birth and death are opposite identicals.

Earth-womb experiences were usually part of the old initiatory ordeals, but here is chiefly a rather light semblance of a symbolic womb-state. Its main feature is acceptance of living among humanity on Earth, and intention of going through Earthlife according to the Pattern which has been learned during the self-sojourn in spiritual dimensions. So eventually is it hoped to equate Heaven and Earth in order to live beyond necessity of either. Therefore the Womb is symbolically entered and emerged from with a new determination to deal with everything encountered on Earth levels in that Spirit which has been achieved by the experience so recently undergone. It is implied that the individual now re-entering incarnatory involvement with living is a much improved version of the one who previously passed this point in the opposite direction. A change of consciousness ought to have occurred on impact with Inner energies which will alter the spiritual awareness of that soul to a marked degree of discernment.

The Magical Symbol of this event is the Cord. Why so? Because it binds a being to Life, conjoins consciousness in the Circle of Cosmos, ties up everything with Truth, and signifies our umbilical connection with Universal Entity. The Cord is generally red, to indicate the line of Blood forming a bond between an individual and his remote ancestry springing from spiritual sources. It might even be thought of as the "tie of Tradition".

Cords and birth have always gone together. Apart from the obvious umbilical link, there is the need to tie this cord with the first ligature or knot met with in Earthlife. Such a knot needs to be secure before the cord is severed, or life may be endangered. So should we tie ourselves firmly with Will so that we "hold together" sufficiently to make Inner living a secure proposition also. At one time by the bed of a birthing woman, all knots and fastenings had to be untied in order to release a life struggling to enter this world. The moment this life appeared in person, however, a "Lifeknot" was fastened upon its own cord in order to secure its tenuous hold on a human habitation. To "bind and loose" is a cord function interpretable in a multitude of ways.

The myth of the maze comes in here. It should be remembered that the Magic thread or Cord had to be cast so that it unravelled by itself and guided the investigator correctly through all the intricacies and problems

THE ROLLRIGHT RITUAL ROUND

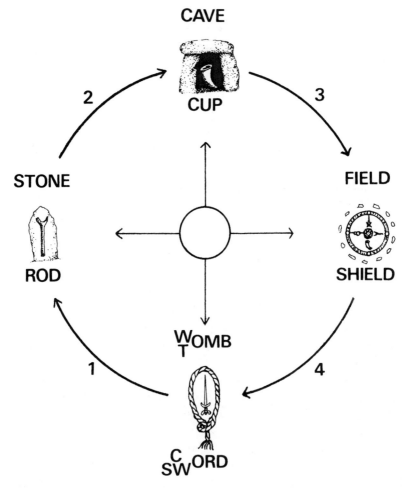

© Wm. G. GRAY 1974

of the bewildering paths so that the central objective was reached safely, the mission of the journey accomplished, and a return route negotiated smoothly. Throughout the entire enterprise, the Cord acted as a guide-line and conductor. In modern terms this could be compared with the lines of colour guiding travellers through the complexities of an Underground rail system. As the Cord is considered Magically here, it signifies the clue of Inner consciousness we ought to start unrolling at birth so that it goes just ahead of us all the way through Earthlife and leads us safely past every peril until our lifework has been accomplished. Then it continues to guide us safely and soundly back to the entry point which has now turned into a take-off platform for Inner Space.

Pilgrims through the Path of Life here in this world need the equivalent of such a Cord very much. Perhaps it may be thought of as a kind of "rolled up" message gathered during Otherlife experience which if it unravels ahead of us here will lead us through Life securely. A genetic inheritance maybe, that will show us how to live if we follow its Inner instructions. Or a roll of tape recorded in other Life-dimensions which tells us all we need to know about living here if we play it back at the right speed on a suitable mechanism. All this symbolism has to be equated with the facilities to be found in our own consciousness and put into practise accordingly. Casting Cords is an old Magical custom to be observed in terms of today's amenities. The elemental attribution of the Cord-Symbol is "Truth", and this is precisely what we should be seeking through Life on either side of this Tomb-Womb point.

Assuming that the Rollright round has been followed faithfully as per layout plan, we are out of the complex and facing Earth-existence again. What now? The same as before. Life presents the same problems and peculiarities whether we meet it on material or metaphysical levels. We have only to adapt the spiritual scheme we should have learned during discarnation and apply it appropriately to mundane matters. Far easier said than done, but it is amazing where patient persistence for life after life will lead in the end.

If at this point it can be taken that our backs are to the Rollright Plan, and its Stations are to be projected ahead through an Earthlife scheme, the application seems perfectly plain. Reading from left to right again we have first the Stone-Rod signifying the early part of life in which codes of conduct should be imparted, discipline instilled, and an ethical standard adopted. Then we have the Cave-cup in which the beautiful Mystery of Love ought to be experienced so that a sense of Divinity may be reached if only for one instant. Even the single Magical touch of that moment should be sufficient to carry a sentient soul for the rest of its round with the most blessed of memories. It seems such a shame so many mortals obliterate this incredible opportunity in their stampede for shoddy and imitation supermarket sex. After the Cave-Cup comes the Field-Shield, that general Circle of companionship which everyone shares throughout human society. This again is composed of Family and personal Stones to signify all the Life classifications of Faiths, countries, races, and every difference constituting a whole community of distinct and developing individuals. After an experience in that Field suitably served by a reliable Shield, it only remains to track along to this very point which has now turned into a Tomb-Gate. Then the entire procedure is repeated along Inner lines of Life. It may be noticed the whole affair is similar to a Moebius strip, and that the "figure of eight" is an Eternity Symbol.

Such is a very generalised outline of the Rollright Ritual background. So much is capable of coming from it that it seems almost incredible what emerges out of each entire celebration. The actual Rite itself is built up from normal ritual procedures, but the verbal structure is of considerable interest. This takes a question-answer form interspersed by brief recitations of the most condensed and concentrated type of consciousness possible. Words are short and meaning long as Life. It was rather strange how laconic and compressed the original conveyance of this verbal framework was. Almost as if the briefest word-symbols with the maximum of Inner spiritual significance were being most carefully selected. Nothing flowery or rhapsodic whatever. Terse, tight, deep and deliberate, powerfully profound, and entirely basic to the business of living according to fundamental formulae. There was an impression of force being folded more and more back into itself so that it appeared in its most compressed state of form.

In a sense, the Rite may be taken to represent any human soul asking vital questions of Life and obtaining the answers it needs by looking inside itself. In another way, it could be supposed that the Spirit of Life were demanding intelligent answers from every living creature faced by the problems posed at every point. At all events the Rite is a very individualistic affair altogether. It calls for comprehension on the deepest possible levels of understanding reachable by participants. However many people participate, they all have to be dealt with one by one as they go round. Only when actually in the Field, may they associate freely with each other and live as they will together. Otherwise, the Rite amounts to a conducted tour of Cosmic truth. Beyond the actual wording of the script, nothing should be said until the Field is reached. Then everything can come out within sensible confines of the social code accepted by all present.

The tempo of the Rite is somewhat slow. No responses are to be given without time for careful thought concerning them. The actual wording should be employed only as a symbol for conveying a whole chain of consciousness connected therewith. This may seem rather ponderous, but it is the only way the Rite can be worked so as to connect with the Spirit which constructed it as a Symbol of Cosmos. "Talk least, think most" was given as a guide for its action throughout.

It is relatively simple for any one individual to get through the Ritual by himself, taking his own time, and pausing at each point long enough to absorb whatever Inner influence was available. Two people can work the Rite very well indeed between them and even alternate the parts of querist and querent. If any greater number were to operate the Ritual, the only practical way would be for each Station to have its special Officer, whose duty it is to deal with all comers as they approach along individual courses. After the last one passes a point, the Officer of the point may then follow behind until everyone except the Officer waiting in attendance at the Womb-Gate is gathered into the Field-Circle safely. This particular Officer then represents the "odd one out", which has a very deep mystical meaning in Cosmic computation.

There are no especial costume demands for the Rite, although if attendance is sufficient, the Officers of the Stations should have some mark to indicate their function. Each will bear their appropriate symbolic Instruments in whatever form seems suitable or acceptable to company present. Otherwise there is no particular need for any equipment which cannot be carried around on the persons of the performers. Of course, there are quite a lot of small, but significant, customs which are bound to come quite naturally to people working this Rite on a number of occasions. They are purely personal concerns to be adopted or omitted according to feeling. An annual offering of elder pieces tied with red thread or ribbon for instance. Or striking around the Stone Circle with cord-ends or sticks. All sorts of little "spiritual intimacies" which grow up with every Life-relationship of this nature.

At each point of the Ritual, "tokens" are exchanged between the Guardian and the Waygoer. These may be absolutely anything at all which are felt to be in keeping with the event. They have to depend entirely on the ingenuity and inventiveness of those concerned, since they are supposed to evoke an Inner response from the deep levels of approach. The tokens may be physical, such as small suggestively shaped stones, characters traced on cards, even twisted pieces of metal or other minor artifacts. On the other hand, they may be made in the form of hand gestures, mimed attitudes, or any symbolic behaviour indicative of how this particular point is being considered. Tokens may be almost anything other than aural or sonic. The reason for this is because they are meant to open other avenues of awareness than those responsive to purely sonic stimuli. The Officer of the Station is supposed to be capable of taking each token, considering it, then returning it to the Waygoer in a slightly different manner so as to present a significant problem for subconscious solution much later on. This is the "unanswered question" which should be taken away from each point for subsequent link-ups with Inner intelligence. If this is not a practical proposition, then a small stone may be picked up in the first instance, borne to the next point where it is replaced by another gathered there, and so on to complete the whole course. The main idea is to impress upon deep levels of consciousness that some notion of especial spiritual importance is brought to each Station, there altered by the "spirit" or indwelling Inner intelligence concerned, and returned to the bearer for later learning. If tokens can be carefully constructed and dealt with, they form a very valuable part of the Rite indeed. Individual ritualists may just place their chosen tokens briefly down at each point, then take them away afterwards in the hope of gathering Inner information by meditational means. One single token presented in various ways will actually serve right round the Rollright course.

It should scarcely be necessary to say that this Ritual does not have to be worked at the Rollrights themselves at all. It is the pattern which matters far more than the place. Once this pattern is understood and formulated, the Rite may be worked anywhere at all, even in the mind without moving a bodily muscle. Of course it is pleasing to perform it if only once at the actual site, but it can be equally effective anywhere else if conditions are right. Far better, in fact, to perform the Rite well in a small room than make a stupid mess of it on the site of the Stones. All this would need is four corners of the room to represent the stations. With imaginative effort, the four Stations could perfectly well be followed in the same place. It is the Inner adjustments which are of greatest importance. Any competent ritualist should be able to work the Rite expertly without even visiting the Rollrights physically at all.

For the sake of practicability the script of the Ritual will be given as a whole section without any comments beyond strictly necessary directions. Then a detailed commentary and run-down can be made afterwards, and various points expanded or investigated. To begin at the beginning, it must be supposed the querent is standing on the edge of a symbolical grave cut in the ground. On the opposite side is the Officer wielding a drawn Sword or knife. Then Inner action commences.

CHAPTER SIX

THE ROLLRIGHT RITUAL

TOMB

Q. WHO IS HERE?

A. I AM . . . *(Name).*

Q. HOW ASK YOU?

A. LEAVE OF LIFE TO LIVE.

Q. WOMBS GIVE, TOMBS TAKE. WHAT WILL YOU?

A. BIDDANCE BY BOTH AS SUMMONED IN THE CIRCLE.

Q. WITH WHAT ENTITLEMENT?

A. MY TRUST IN TRUTH, AND BY THIS TOKEN.

(token dealt with)

Q. TAKEN, TURNED, AND TENDERED.

A. THANKS BE TO YOU.

BE BODY BORNE BY GRAVE
YET SWORD SHALL SPIRIT SAVE
BY BRIDGING THE ABYSS
WITH FINEST PATH TO BLISS.
(death and revival mime)
ONCE DEAD, TWICE ALIVE.
FALL, REST, RISE, THRIVE!

IF YOU WOULD GROW LIKE A GOD
SEEK OUT THE SECRET OF THE ROD.

A. FROM HERE TO WHERE?

Q. WHERE STONE WHICH LAY ON MOTHER EARTH
NOW POINTS ANOTHER WAY TO BIRTH.

STONE

Q. WHO STANDS?

A. I.

Q. WHAT FOR?

A. MY BIRTHRIGHT.

Q. WHAT HOLDS YOU?

A. HOPE.

Q. UNTIL WHAT END?

A. UNTIL THAT STONE IS DUST, AND THEN FOREVER.

Q. WHAT RAISES HOPES SO HIGH?

A. GOD, BLOOD, AND ROD.

Q. HOW CLAIM YOU?

A. BY MY LIFE AND THIS TRUE TOKEN.

(token dealt with)

Q. TAKEN, TURNED, AND TENDERED.

A. THANKS BE TO YOU.

Q. AS UPRIGHT ROD AND STANDING STONE
LIVE ONLY TO ONE END ALONE.
BETWEEN ALL EARTH AND HEAVEN BE
THE RULER OF YOUR DESTINY.
(rod mime)
LET RULE BE SURE AND STRAIGHT
AN HONEST SIMPLE GUIDE.
BY EVERY QUARTER-GATE
BE IT FORTH CRIED

(here the Calls are sounded to the Quarters around the Stone and repeated by hearers).

East. HOLD HU.

South. HAIL ALL.

West. HARM NONE.

North. HOLD I.

Q. IF YOU WOULD REACH HIGHER UP
SEEK OUT THE SECRET OF THE CUP.

A. HOW THENCE FROM HENCE?

Q. WHERE SACRED CAVERN IS CONCEALED
FOR MYSTERIES TO BE REVEALED.

CAVE

Q. WHO ARE YOU?

A. ONE OF NONE.

Q. WHAT WILL YOU?

A. NAUGHT.

Q. WHAT OFFER YOU?

A. ALL I AM.

Q. UNTO WHOM?

A. WHOSO LOVES MOST.

Q. WHY?

A. THAT I MAY BLESSED BE.

Q. HOW EARN YOU ENTITY?

A. BY LIFELOVE, AND THIS TOKEN.

(the token dealt with)

Q. TAKEN, TURNED, AND TENDERED.

A. THANKS BE TO YOU.

Q. IN HOLIEST HOLE
OUR WHOLE IS HIDDEN.
NOW, FOR SAKE OF SOUL
ARE WE CUP-BIDDEN.
(shows empty Cup)
AN EMPTY CUP ALONE CAN FILL.
WITH PERFECT LOVE, BE AS YOU WILL.

(fills Cup with wine)

BLESSED BE WINE
AS BLOOD DIVINE.

(elevates Cup and invokes Deity)

WHOEVER THOU MAY BE,
MAKE THIS OUR DRINK
A LIVING LINK
WITH THINE IDENTITY.

(offers Cup to drink)

MAY WHAT WE SEEK BE FOUND
IN PERFECT PEACE PROFOUND.

(silence and stillness. Presently the Cup is filled with water)

WHEN WE MAY NOT BE MORE
THEN LET OUR LIVES OUTPOUR
IN BLESSEDNESS TO EARTH
BY VIRTUE OF OUR BIRTH.

(water libated to ground)

Q. IF NOW YOU WOULD FIND MORE AFIELD,
SEEK OUT THE SECRET OF THE SHIELD.

A. WHITHER FROM HITHER?

Q. WHERE CIRCLING STONES A SAFEGUARD SPAN
THAT WARMLY WELCOMES GOD AND MAN.

FIELD

Q. WHO BE YE?

A. I AM ME.

Q. WOULD YE BE ONE OF WE?

A. IF I MAY BE.

Q. WHO ARE WE?

A. MY FRIENDS AND FAMILY.

Q. WHAT BRING YE TO WE?

A. ANOTHER AS WE WILL.

Q. IF WE RECEIVE YE, HOW BELIEVE YE?

A. BY FELLOWFAITH, AND THIS ITS TOKEN.

(token dealt with)

Q. TAKEN, TURNED, AND TENDERED.

A. THANKS BE TO YOU.

Q. FOR HARMONY TO HOLD THE FIELD,
ALL MUST UPHOLD ITS ONLY SHIELD
BY HONOURING A SIMPLE PLEDGE
PROCLAIMED AROUND ITS OUTER EDGE.
"I WILL TRY TO BE
UNTO MY BROTHERS
AS I WOULD ALL OTHERS
TRULY WERE TO ME."
IF WITH THIS YE WILL AGREE,
WELCOME AND BE ONE OF WE.

A. *(lays hand on Shield)*
BY THIS SHIELD I SWEAR
TO KEEP OUR FAITH IN CARE.

Q. COME IN AND BE
AT HOME WITH WE.

(Entertainment now held in Circle-Field. This special ROLLRIGHT Song goes to a traditional air.)

THE ROLLRIGHT SONG

1. Come gather together in Circles of Stone.
   Why stay outside sadly and live all alone?
   When here is a fire and feeding as well,
   With dancing and song and good stories to tell.

Chorus
Set the Stones a-rolling right,
Follow up with all our might.
Let them circle day and night,
Going round the way of Light.

2. In Circles we live, and by circles we learn
   How things go together each one in its turn.
   Our future before us grows out of the past.
   Where we came from at first we shall go to at last.

Chorus

3. What can we ask for while living on Earth
   That makes any meaning to death and re-birth?
   Our lives are so short and our Stones stay so long
   We must hope they will hold and re-echo our song.

Chorus

4. So large is this world and so little are we
   That Stones offer safety as much as may be.
   While the blessings we pray for to make us feel big
   Are flags, fodder, flax, and a good deal of frig!

Chorus

5. Some people join us and other ones go,
   We may not be clever, but this much we know.
   Whoever attempts to set up on his own
   Had better begin with a Circle of Stone.

Chorus

6. As Moon circles Earth while the Earth circles Sun,
   Let us stay close together until we are one.
   Friendly and happy, with head, heart, and hand,
   In our Circles of Stone for as long as they stand.

Chorus

(the closing of the Circle may be given by any chosen member.)

ONE AND ALL, GOOD FAITHFUL FRIENDS
THERE COMES A TIME ENJOYMENT ENDS.
SO LET US GLADLY GO FROM HERE
TO WORK THE WILL WHICH WAITS ELSEWHERE.
OUR FAITH WAS SHARED, OUR FEAST WAS SERVED,
AND ANCIENT CUSTOMS WERE OBSERVED.
SWORDS GOT SHARPENED, RODS UPRAISED,
CUPS BEEN DRUNK, AND OLD ONES PRAISED.
WE KEPT OUR PROMISE WITH THE SHIELD,
SO PEACE PREVAILED INSIDE OUR FIELD.
WORDS WERE SAID, AND WILLS WERE TRIED,
PLEDGES MADE, AND TRUE KNOTS TIED.
NAMES WERE CALLED AND STONES WERE STRUCK,
LOVE WAS LINKED WITH LIFE AND LUCK.
THE HORN WAS BLOWN AROUND THE STONE,
AND FIRE WAS LIT WITH WIND AND WIT.
NO MORE TO DO
THANKS BE TO YOU
UNTIL WE GREET
WHEN NEXT WE MEET.
NAUGHT LEFT TO TELL,
SAVE—FARE YE WELL:

(members now quit Circle informally and singly. They are challenged at the last Station.)

WOMB

Q. WHO GOES WHERE?

A. A TRAVELLER TO TRUTH.

Q. KNOW YOU THE WAY?

A. I KNOW IT NOT.

Q. KNOT MAKES NOTHING.

(cord noose mime.)

OUT OF NIL
COMES ALL YOU WILL
IN DUE ACCORD
WITH WILL AND WORD
TAKE THIS CORD AND TIE
YOUR SELF TO LIFE FOR AYE.
MAY IT LEAD YOU THROUGH
WHATEVER COMES TO YOU.

(womb entry mime.)

GO FORTH AGAIN BY EARTH
CONTINUE WITH YOUR BIRTH.
OUR MOTHER'S KINDLY WOMB
AFFORDS YOU READY ROOM.
SO LIVE ONE ONCE MORE AND LEARN
HOW YOU MAY BEST RETURN.
GOOD BE WITH YOU.

A. AND WITH YOU TOO.

(womb-leaver rises, makes gesture of embracing Existence and cries):

HAIL ALL OF EARTH AND SKY!
LIFE SPIRIT! KNOW ME! HERE COME I!

CHAPTER SEVEN

THE SENSE OF THE SCRIPT

Brief as the bare words are, they carry a mass of meaning leading to a depth of Inner realisations entirely beyond an ordinary range of understanding. Yet they are very simple. They seem to indicate that the most involved complications of consciousness are only simplicities seen from an awkward angle. To start with, they lead off from the viewpoint of sentient soul about to face a complete change of conscious life altogether. Always a prospect apt to be alarming or disturbing unless there is a virtual certainty of improved and happier circumstances. Even so, there is almost bound to be apprehension or some degree of alerted anticipation. To the initiated, this Rite begins with what is meant for an immediate assurance of: "HU (who) is here."

This one word "Who" has the double meaning of HU, signifying the Great Spirit of Life and Light. It translates literally as: "He (or That) which IS". One might say "God", or any other term indicating Infinite Identity. HU is such an ancient synonym for the Unutterable Name among mankind that the Rollrighters would certainly have recognised it. Here, both God and Man ask each other "Who are you?" How can any human ask the Infinite what or Whom It is, unless that same human is able to tell Infinity in return exactly what and whom he is in himself? The two replies are bound up together in a common answer somewhere in the depths of Universal understanding.

So the human answers, "I AM", and then attaches a name. An initiate would give his "Magical code-name" here instead of his ordinary civil cognomen. The birth-certificate name is what others call any individual, and how they consider that person. A "Magical Name", however, is someone's own secret estimation of himself by conclusions of consciousness reached through facing the Inner facts of his own force-formations. An ordinary name is something people are "thrown into", while the secret "Self-Name" is something which has to be *grown* into. That makes all the difference. Therefore when the ritualist here says "I AM", this means, "My Life-beliefs have led me into being ... (so and so)". I AM is a "God Name" itself. A supreme "God-Name". In the first few words of the Rite, therefore, a direct relationship has been asked and acknowledged between Infinite Individuality, and a finite individual. One might say things have got off to a good (God) start.

To say, "How ask you (HU)?" means "What do you expect Divinity to do for you?" or "What is your Life-Will?" Before anything can be accomplished anywhere, someone or something has to know what is needed. To know what to think of Life and expect from it is an essential prerequisite for living properly. How many people really and truly know what they are actually living for deep down in themselves? How many even bother to look? An initiated individual at least has some clearly conscious ideas on this vital issue. He gives them here as "Leave of Life to live". An assurance by the Life-Spirit within him that he is living in accordance with the intention behind his entire being. That there is, in fact, a point and purpose to everything in his existence which adds up into a single spiritual statement of Self-meaning. The same phrase may also signify leaving one type of life on Earth for a different condition entirely in other dimensions of Cosmos.

The advancing individual is then reminded that Life proceeds back and forth over the same point of entry-departure in this world symbolised by a Tomb or Womb. In or Out. It all depends which side of the same Gate one stands. A hesitant person is often asked the irritated question, "Are you coming or going?" and this is the query here, though entirely without irritation. Just a straight demand to say what is willed and then do it. Have we a choice of Tomb or Womb? Yes, we have, but the way to one lies through the other. If we want to go on living in this world we shall have to find a womb willing to bring us back, which means going through a Tomb to find one. Conversely, if we want to continue living in a state of delighted discarnation, we can only get into this through a Tomb, which entails going in and out of a Womb to reach one. That is Life. In and Out all the time, until the secret of spiritual stabilisation is learned, and we discover how to direct our own Life-courses otherwise to better purpose. So the applicant admits a willingness to tackle both Tomb and Womb as called by the Life-Spirit through the Circle of Cosmos in search of Ultimate Understanding.

Not unsurprisingly, he is then asked by what right or entitlement he expects to continue in this course of living. He replies simply because he trusts in the One Truth (whatever that may be) behind all Being. One might say ultralife. Only "No-one" knows what truth is. It is here admitted to be all that anyone may trust in Life. If the answer to this is "Nothing", the Truth for such a respondent would indeed be—NOTHING! Whatever is absolutely trustworthy to anyone, is Truth for that soul. A complete confidence in Cosmos. What higher Truth is possible for any human?

As evidence of such a trust, the applicant here produces some token to demonstrate his attitude. Something quite simple and sincere, just to show a belief put into some form of practise. This is what the tokens are for. Pledges of purpose. The token is taken, slightly altered, then either returned to the donor, or placed somehow on the point. In practise, if the token is a little stone, it can be put on the ground, if a small piece of ribbon, tied to a tree, or something of that nature. If it happens to be some kind of personal talisman, then it need only be taken, touched to the forehead while thinking is directed into it, and then handed back. There are many ways of working this exchange. The reply, "Thanks be to you" also means "Thanks be to HU (God)", of course.

Now follows an almost Traditional "death and resurrection" drama symbolised by a conventional mime of lying down in a "dead" position, then being restored to living by the Will within the Words heard. This is a custom shared by nearly every School or System which uses ritual in any form. One easy and spiritually valuable way of working it is thus. Lying face down on the Earth or its equivalent, a small hole is dug in the soil with a knife at face level. This is the "grave". Then, cupping the hands round the mouth, all those things which anyone would want to leave behind at bodily death, or bury them out of themselves forever, are whispered very softly into the Earth. The "dead past burying its dead". The worst of oneself being expelled from the best of oneself. An interment of ill-wills and evils. A decent burial of whatever is too bad for inclusion in the new Life ahead. A committal of "corpse consciousness" to the Earth it best belongs with. That done, the soil is smoothed over, and the words of awakening attended to.

These state quite plainly it is only a body which Earth can hold. The Sword-Symbol indicates how the "edge of Inner Life" intersects our ordinary Earth-limited awareness, and its points touch us on many occasions in order to wake us up into wider states of consciousness. We have to keep our attention to the "Inner Awakening" as finely attuned as the edge of a Sword and as sharply focused as its point, if we are to cross the Chasm between our Lifestates of "Here" and "There", and land ourselves successfully on the "Other Side" of Life. During the mime, appropriate gestures with an actual Sword or knife are permissible if sensibly performed.

There is a reminder given that a single death means a doubly significant life. So it does, because the events and effects of that past incarnation have to be equated and evaluated into a self-summation and added to the truth- total which all must become Ultimately. Then the Life- cycle of descent, sojournment, ascent, and attainment is acknowledged. The four-fold changes of consciousness we have to undergo as we travel around Life in search of Truth symbolised by Light. Once that is understood, comes an injunction that if further progress toward the Infinite is intended, it will be necessary to go on still further and learn the secrets bound up with the Symbol of a Rod. The applicant naturally enquires where, and is told to seek a Stone which once lay supine on earth, but has now been raised by human efforts until it points to higher levels of Life altogether.

This makes sound sense. The Stone is a Symbol of Man's first serious attempts to lift himself up from this Earth and point himself in what he believed was the right direction to Divinity of a Cosmic condition of Maximum Manhood. It is no mere accident that the Stone indicates the stars. From far-off stellar space came the seed of human Life to this Earth, and sooner or later we have to go home again. Raising that Stone was a gesture of acknowledgement and Inner recognition towards this beginning and end of Earthlife. It was not only a wave of farewell, but a hailing sign of future fulfilment, too. Now, we might stand another such Symbol beside it in the shape of a space-rocket on a launching-pad. This is the equivalent of our Standing Stone in this century, and it will be surpassed by its offspring in the next. However, if it were possible to see both these symbols side by side, it would be obvious that if the first had not been set up so long ago, the second could not have lifted itself today. In addition to that, the same fundamental faith lies behind both Stone and Starship. As we look at them together, we are seeing a combined example of Man's confidence in Cosmos and his own spiritual status therein.

The Standing Stone still speaks very clearly to Mankind. It has always the same message, which sounds something like, "Stop lying to yourself. Get up, stand on the basis of your best beliefs and look Life in the face. Be unshakably firm, but do not be moved to hurt anyone. Endure. Be strong, patient, and acknowledge nothing above you except Heaven". The Stone has a lot more to tell those who listen carefully. It might also quote, "everything comes to he who waits". That very Stone has stood there for centuries waiting for a Starship to take its place. It may yet be standing when whatever replaces the rocketship lifts the last Man on Earth finally to the stars forever. The same Stone which saw the start of our civilisation may witness the end of it here also. If we survive the Stone, we shall have reached the farthest stars. We may even reach Divinity Itself. That is the story which the Stone has to tell us in our time.

As the oncomer approaches the Stone another challenge is issued. The significance of each challenge is, "In what light do you regard yourself?"

*"Be body borne
by grave,
Yet Sword shall
spirit save."*

This means everyone is expected to declare an estimation of themselves in a single and summative style. At each point of Life another Self-sight will be demanded, and as we see ourselves, so do we become the selves we intend to Know. This is the importance of these interrogatory openings at the commencement of every Station. To make someone see himself in whatever light of belief relates with that particular Life-point. Here the reply is briefly "I". Not only does this stand for Individuality, but is symbolic of a straight line or Rod standing up for itself. This is the right attitude for arrival here.

So what does any "I" stand for apart from Itself? As the script says, a birthright. The entitlement of someone's existence. Everyone gets born for and to some purpose or other, no matter how pointless this may seem to cynical observers. We may never know with our ordinary awareness what our own birthrights are, but they are precisely what we stand for as Individualising entities. A birthright is the most important Inner asset of anyone in incarnation. It is something spiritual we "bring over with us" in order to develop during our Earthlives. Therefore it is acknowledged here.

When asked what holds the seekers to their birthrights, the answer is plainly "Hope". The only word which makes Life bearable on many of its occasions. Take away hope, and what is left? Nothing but the deadliest of endings in the Abyss of the abandoned. Hence, "Abandon Hope all ye who enter here". This is why Despair was termed the deadliest of sins by Christians and pagans alike. Christians qualified this a little by specifying, "Despair of God's Mercy." One might utterly despair of Man, lose hope of this world ever becoming any better, but on no account whatever must hope be lost of Infinite Magnanimity somewhere, somehow, sometime. Only the hold on Life which Hope offers us, will enable us to eventually surmount every single one of its obstacles in the end. We have to out-hope Death, defeat, destruction—everything. The sort of Hope needed here has to transcend all possible human errors and horrors. It must be based much higher than upon any human or material possibility. It has to be a Hope extending far beyond bodily bounds into spiritual states of being. There is no limit to Hope except Ultimate Life Itself. Therefore Hope is obviously our most direct line of connection therewith. Physical death or disaster must be merely incidents in our Hope-lines. It is literally all we have to live for, and the only faculty which will carry us from one end of Life to the other. To lose Hope is tantamount to losing Life altogether. So when the query is raised on how long Hope is likely to be held, the reply reduces the Standing Stone to dust by atmospheric abrasion, and then

"As upright Rod and Standing Stone
Live only to one end alone."

extends to infinity. Hopes have to continue for Life long after Man has quitted his visit to Earth. Where our Hopes can go, we may accompany them.

When asked what raises Hope so high, the intensely significant reply of "God, Blood, and Rod" is given. God is to be understood as the individual's concept of Divinity, or his own Ultimate Lifestate. The Hope of Godhood is the highest Man may possibly have. The word "Blood" means that inherent Lifeline of spiritual genetics which makes us all "Children of Cosmos." It is the "Blood-Royal" we all hope to inherit or acquire through our associations with what may as well be frankly termed the "Inner aristocracy." All human life is eligible for such an honour if earned. Those who gain it, gain the Holy Grail, that high Hope of every Initiate understanding this Mystery. Then the term "Rod". Apart from the Magical Instrument symbolism, it also signifies "Rede", or counsel of faith. Having a "right rede" or creed, gives anyone a Hope of everything making Life worth while. Again the word can mean "Root", or the very stems of our spiritual structure deriving from divinity. What better hopes can people have than those of sound roots going back right to the very bedrock of their beings? If we take the word as "Rood", it calls up the Cross Tree, or Life Tree of living sacrifice. This is essentially the Hope of Man from every angle. Altogether the one word "Rod" here produces a multitude of meanings, and there are more yet for those to find who are capable of delving deeper.

Anyone claiming to hold such high Hopes had better have some very substantial backing for this. On being asked, the entrant says truthfully that Life itself is the best reason for having Hope at all, and so indeed it is. Not necessarily Life on this Earth at all, but the Principle of Life for what it is, and what it is worth to the respondent. A token is offered to represent such a statement, and after being accepted, considered, and suitably treated, is dealt with accordingly. The Divinity is thanked both *per se*, and in the person of the Officer. To recognise the presence of Divinity somewhere in another human being, however remotely, is a feature of this Rite. The double meaning You and Hu, is of great mystical importance.

Here follows some Rod miming, when the movements of a physical Rod can be made to represent something of spiritual significance in the hands of a competent operator. It should certainly illustrate the point of the admonition given with it. The hearer is clearly told to live as the Stone and Rod Symbols show. In an upright and steadfast manner, guiding his own destiny toward Divinity. How else? It is also stressed that a straight and simple rule of Life be adopted and borne around the course of living, much as a Rod or Staff might assist an ordinary journey. So important is it to have such a definite Life-rule, that it should be called to the Four Quarters so that Humanity and Divinity alike may hear and witness. The Rule, Rede, or Creed is then delivered in this manner. Traditionally it should be accompanied by blasts from a horn, and this positively does emphasise it in a way nothing else seems to. The Rede is fourfold.

HOLD HU. This means to hold and acknowledge a Divinity, here conceived as Infinite Being associated with the Principle of Light and Life. Without this prerequisite, nothing else can follow in any kind of Faith.

HAIL ALL. This greets the whole of Creation as the Life companions of the believer. The Brotherhood of BEING. It also means Hale, in the sense of "may everyone be well and fit". A sort of universal well-wishing or "Good-greeting" which relates the believer beneficently all round. Again it means Heal, or an intention of righting wrongs and restoring health and harmony among all living beings in need. Then it signifies Hele, an old word meaning to respect holy confidences and keep them sacred in sensible secrecy. In other words, "be cautious", a very good admonition in any life.

HARM NONE. This says exactly what it means. To do no deliberate harm to any living creature. It was once put "living harmlessly". Minding one's own business might be a homely way of putting things here.

HOLD I. An affirmation that these principles are what the declarant intends to uphold throughout Life. An acknowledgement and acceptance of all they stand for, and a declaration that they will be borne as a standard or rule for living by. That they are the Golden Rule, and will be treated deservedly.

This certainly seems as good a way of categorising a Creed as any other. It embraces the "Do unto others" idea, and generally puts all the fundamentals of the great creeds already followed into a very neat nutshell. In seven very simple words, it says, "I believe in God, Man, and Myself." What else *is* there to believe in as a Way of Life?

There is an interesting point here concerning the old "Calls" which used to be sounded from hill-tops or other naturally sacred sites. The idea was to use some definite sonic resonance and "call" or chant it in such a way that the whole "spirit of the place" responded. The Caller would sound off whatever it was, and then immediately afterwards everyone listened intently inside themselves for an answering echo bringing them important Inner information. Perhaps a relic of this now is the muezzin's call from a minaret. The difficulty of making any such call work today, is the necessity for human silence following the sonic. Only Nature has to answer. An answer to these Calls can only be heard in self-silence against a quiet background of perfectly natural noises such as wind, water, birds, etc. Every day this becomes less possible amid the motorised madness of mankind. Still, there can yet be found occasional opportunities for "Calling the Creed" and "Listening to Life."

After this acceptance of creed controlled conduct as a Life-standard, the wayseeker is told that any hopes of living on yet higher levels are bound up with a great Mystery concerning a Cup, which will be revealed in connection with a Cavern. Cups and Caverns should be familiar Symbols to most initiated intelligences, but they should never be taken as merely sexual significances only. They go much deeper than that. A Christian here would immediately see the Incarnation and Eucharist implied. A Celt might recognise the Cauldron of Ceridwen, or sacred vessel in which the whole of Life gets boiled down to a single meaning in the shape of a Golden Drop. It may be the Cauldron into which dead heroes are thrown so that they came back to Life in new and finer forms. However the Cavern and Cup are considered, there is always the theme of regeneration, renewal, and good new Life coming out of old and outworn entities. Eternal Existence, bubbling or pouring straight out of its Source with all the energy and enthusiasm of an inexhaustible Identity.

The most sacred parts of most ancient Mysteries were usually conducted in a Cavern. Apart from the sonics, privacy, and dramatic conditions, a Cavern represents the "Holy Hollow" or Zoic Zero of that Infinite Nil out of which ALL emerges. A "Cavern" is nothing in the midst of something", and this is the principle to be approached here. Being "something" ourselves, we think that "nothing" is there. So it is, but what is "nothing" to us, is ALL to Inner states of Identity. So the Cavern, and its concomitant of the Cup, is a very sacred Symbol altogether. When we are able to recognise the highest kind of life in a state which seems to us like Silence and Stillness, we shall be approaching the Infinite on something resembling Its own terms.

This point is emphasised by the challenge and its odd response, "One of none." All enumeration begins with Zero, and every individual is some *one* who originally emerged from None. Here, this relationship

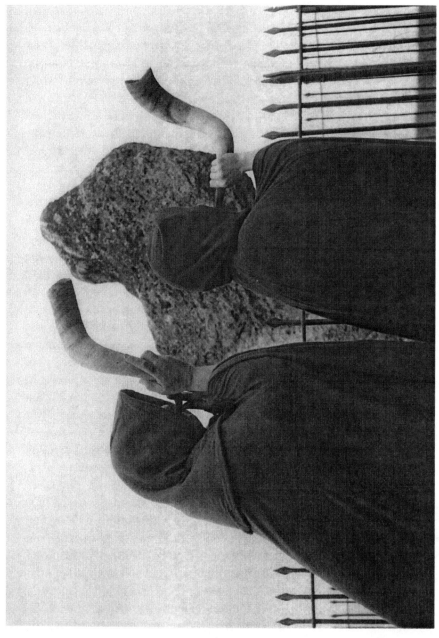

*"The horn was
blown
Around the
Stone."*

is clearly recognised and admitted. Its ultimate outcome is claimed with will. Nothing is willed. The metaphysical meaning of this is profound. To intend Nothing is to affirm All. The Zero point is a poising position from which the will may be directed anywhere in Life at all. To will Nothing means *anything* may be attempted. The importance of comprehending what Nothing signifies here, cannot be over-emphasised.

In order to gain this Nothing, all the "I Am"-ness of an individual is offered. All I AM to become I AM NOT. This is really no more than everyone asks for all the time. We are never satisfied with what we are, and always demand of Life that we should become this, that, or the other instead. That is the way we are made, and if only we demanded to become more worthwhile people instead of mere possessors of more property, Life would be a better proposition entirely. Here, the Ultimate demand upon Divinity is made. "Make me so much that I will need only Nothing." Once this was put, "Cast out desire". It can be interpreted as, "let me possess Nothing but Perfect Peace Profound." The whole concept here has so much meaning it is capable of untold expansion.

The point arises, however, to whom or what is All to be offered. There has to be a recipient somewhere to accept any kind of an offering. The answer comes unequivocally—such a supreme sacrifice may only be made to whom or whatever is capable of maximum Love. Certainly no human being could possibly achieve more than the slightest attempt at loving in the real sense of the term. What we sometimes call love is but the feeblest flicker in imitation of the real Actuality. There is only one Great Lover alive, and that is the Life-Spirit Itself. To be in love with Life is the most wonderful experience any human may have, and if this reflects through another human, then they have both been very highly blessed indeed, as the Rite admits at this point. What can be more blessed in Life than Love?

Blessings are best earned, however, and so the aspirant is asked how the right to a living entity may be deserved. The reply is by "Lifelove", of which a token is tendered. This composite term does not mean only "love of Life", which is quite natural to every creature. It also signifies a life spent in loving activities or affairs motivated by love. It does not specify the objectives of such love, because these differ according to individuals, and besides, love does not have to have objectives at all except itself. To love for Love's sake is an ability all mystics and Initiates aim to achieve. Why should we have to wait for something or someone to specially love? Why not just love, and find a focal point for this finest of Forces when and as opportunity arrives. Why not again simply Love, and let what wills be the beloved? This is true Lifelove as implied here. Whatever its token may be for anyone, is duly tendered and disposed of with thanks to Divinity for the dispensation.

Now follows what amounts to a Communion Rite in which partakers share the Blessed Blood they would belong with. This act of establishing a voluntary blood-relationship with Deity is far, far older than any Christian commemoration. It goes right back to the very origins of our arrival on Earth, and past that point yet. In early Earthtimes, it was believed that only chosen Kings could attain this blood-contact, but once secured, it might be passed along down a line of succession among more ordinary, though still selected, mortals. How far this connects with primitive people forming blood-relationships with far superior cultures from other planets, and then propagating the species, is uncertain. Even so, those advanced beings who might seem like Gods to primitives here, still had their own origins to account for, and must have descended from a higher blood-line themselves. So does one Blood ultimately unite all creatures of Cosmos. It is this identical Blood, or Life-line with our Primal Progenitor which is symbolically shared here. That is the Holy Grail. Here, Man is recognising his Mother-Father-Maker by claiming kinship through ties of Lifeblood which bind all beings into one Family.

The line: "In Holiest Hole our Whole is hidden" is of utmost significance. It indicates the Infinity of Nil containing the entirety of All as a Cup holds its contents. The whole of Consciousness in Cosmos contained and concealed by an Indefinable Absolute Awareness. It also speaks of the Divine Mother-Deep or "Cosmic cervix" of which every conceivable Life in Creation comes. That Mother-Mystery universally acknowledged by a Lifelove much too deep for any words. "She whose speech is Silence, and whose movement Motionless." That for which we have to make room in our hearts at this moment, and so construct the Inner Cup whose outer Symbol we are now considering.

It is next said that we are Cup-bidden for the sake of our souls. Not minds or intellects, but souls. Our abilities to feel, appreciate, and empath with Living existence. Our capabilities of contacting Cosmos by sheer love and devotion. Thinking and reasoning are quite incapable of embracing any concept of Divinity at this Life-level. Nothing but a spiritual capacity to "take in Truth" by entering it with pure love can be of service here. This is what "soul" means in the context here. A soul does not argue, think, talk, or otherwise arrange units of consciousness. It either accepts or rejects as it will. Here, we have to accept the Cup of Life containing the ingredients of our immortality just as it is offered to us. No less, because there can be no more for anyone.

The Symbol of an Empty Cup is then considered. But is it really empty? Anything may be in Nothing. What is emptiness except anticipation of All? Once more the lesson is presented that in order to be filled by Divinity, everything else has to be emptied out. The Symbol of an empty Cup (or Room) has so much meaning to be meditated upon that this alone would fill all the cranium cups present. If it is remembered that some of the first Cups used here were skulls, the significance of an empty Cup will grow deeper. Suppose it were possible to empty out a mind then re-fill it entirely with much better ideas? Nothing to do with so-called "brainwashing", but a deliberate and direct effort by the Being behind that mind to get rid of useless mental matter and replace this with an improved collection of consciousness. Then again, what if the spirit behind the soul were able to pour out any poisonous tendencies and restock this void with more suitable spiritual contents? The Empty Cup has many such lessons to teach.

Now comes a "Master Concept" or Key to the Operation. "With Perfect Love; Be as you will." Perfect love is only possible in a supremely spiritual state of Life. It is here considered as a human attempt to act in a Godlike manner, because none but Divinity can Love perfectly. Nevertheless, it is advised to make the best possible attempt in this direction. The admonition to "Be as you (HU) will", means becoming as Hu-in-You wills. That is to say the will of Divinity working through the human extension of that will in a human agent. Perfect Love working as It wills in this, or any other world. Put another way, "Thy will be done in earth as it is in Heaven", or, "As above—so below."

Here follows a benediction of the wine representing that Blood which is meant to bind all Being together into one indissoluble Brotherhood and Faith-family of Life. The Kinship of Kings, or Blood-Royal by which our direct relationship with Divinity is established. The Grace of the Grail. The Lifelink with Infinite Identity. This is done by the simplest sort of faith-formula. Just a hopeful and confident statement that the wine-Symbol be acceptable in the same spirit as if it actually were what it represents. There is no kind of transubstantiation whatsoever implied. The wine remains physically wine and nothing else on that level. Conceptually, however, a change does, or should, happen. What ought to alter is the conscious attitude of recipients. If the Inner acceptance of that wine-Symbol changes to accommodate it *as if* it were really and truly the Sacred Blood which would indeed bring immortality and relationship with Divinity, then so it becomes spiritually for partakers. While not being a material transubstitution, it truly is a spiritual transfusion for those who transform it into this by the force of faith.

"Blessed be wine
As Blood Divine."

Lifting the Cup and its content towards the Light, a most moving metrical invocation is now made. With the deepest possible sincerity, Deity is asked as the Ultimate Life whose Name can never be known by Man, to be conscious of this Cup and contents, and confirm what it is believed to be—a Lifelink with Its own immortal identity. There should be a sufficient pause here for everyone concerned to adjust Inwardly with this idea and "bring it through" into believable degrees of discernment. This is where the ability to suspend disbelief must be employed with maximum effort. No matter what physical perceptions say, or critical consciousness remarks, such limited viewpoints simply have to be spiritually superseded at this instant, and the closest sense of communion with the Cosmic Spirit of Life accepted as an actuality. This is accomplished by a process of Inner identification, and pushing past the point of unbelief as far as possible along this one line of linkage with Infinite Life.

The wine-Blood Symbol is shared in the hope of Ultimate Union with Perfect Peace Profound or the "Light beyond all Life." The highest hope we may possibly have. Symbolically, partakers should become aware of *belonging* to a Faith-family extending not only through closest companions, but entirely throughout the whole of Creation. They ought to feel and *know* "Life and we are One." There are no words to speak of this certainty, and not the slightest item of intelligence to substantiate it. Only those who have it may hold it, and they may only salute their secret in silence. Being of one Blood, they no longer have to believe. They truly Belong.

So here follows a Silence for a short while. When the Officiant judges a return to the Rollright round should be made, the pouring of water into the Cup is a gracefully gentle signal. Speaking softly, a reminder is given that the point of no-return has been passed, and now it is time to continue with this Inner Life-course back in the general direction of re-birth. A libation is made to the Earth as a sign of Sky-seed commencing its descent, and in memory of our Ocean-mother who engendered the organisms out of which our human bodies had to be built. Having touched the highest apex of awareness we were able to reach, we now have to come steadily and carefully down to Earthlife again by the Ladder of Life communicating therewith.

Wayfarers are told that another Station awaits their company before birth becomes imminent. The sign of this is a Circle of safety and security symbolised by a Shield. Here all are welcome who come in the name of God and Man together. This is where everyone can be happy together and sort themselves into family and other groupings best suited for individual or intended developments. A kind of celestial convention as it were, for mutual adjustment and arrangement of living souls into whatever categories of Life seem most likely to advance their spiritual evolution. No impositions are forced on them by any kind of imperative Deity; they have to work everything out among each other and come to what conclusions they reach by means of the Inner initiative inspired in them by their Blood-contacts with the Cosmic ancestry they now share in common.

This Shielded Circle, or Family Field, is not merely a muddled mêlée of Mankind where everyone is thrown into one untidy heap to struggle for survival. A Field of this type signifies security of its society, solely because it is a self-selective safeguard for spiritually inclined individuals to live and work together along their combined level of Inner consciousness. There is nothing discriminative about this whatever. It means that at any level of Life whatever, humans are happiest and most harmonious when they find what might be described as their natural habitat. Differing types of people need different sorts of environment and facilities if they are to be at their best. This does not mean they have to stay in such positions forever, unless, of course, they insist for some perverse purpose they are quite entitled to have, providing they do not try and inflict it upon unwilling undeserving entities.

The spiritual situation here is that everyone should discover their own proper places for their present Life-points, and gravitate thereto quite naturally and normally. This means finding their rightful Faith-families, or whatever intimate circles of other individuals they are most closely connected with by Truth-ties and Life-links. Just as we all have physical relatives on Earth, so do we belong with specific "Inner families" Otherwhere. To each, his own. No more nor less than that. Each distinct family is here symbolised by an especial Stone bearing a distinguishing device, and the entire Family Field is covered with a shared Shield symbolising the Faith in Life they all agree upon entirely. That particular point of agreement is thus both a covenant held in common among them, and a guarantee of their good-will toward one another.

It will be noted there is a curious change of tone here. The Rite becomes not exactly "folksy", but there is an odd touch of rusticity in the speech. This was quite intentional. The "country angle" is meant to indicate an unvarnished basic honesty of approach and a blunt belief that Life should bring out the best in everyone by perfectly natural processes encouraged with human husbandry. Man works better with, and not in defiance of Nature. Rustically conscious people usually respect this rule more than urbanites. Hence the alteration of angle. Besides, the Rollrights are connected with a country Tradition deriving from the deepest possible roots in the grounds of our most fundamental fertility. Humans are apt to forget that their civilisations stem from the soil which provides their food, clothes, minerals, and natural necessities. All the rest of our artifacts are relatively ephemeral. One world-wide cataclysm wiping out the majority of Mankind would send survivors where they belonged, and they would have to start scratching a living from the bare earth again—if they were capable. Civilisations have risen and fallen in this world already, but the "soul of the soil", or pattern of Life on which the Rollrights are based, will always be here whether humans exist to follow it or not. That is its intrinsic value for today and forever.

This Station, therefore, begins by an identity check as usual, but the reply is only "Me," as someone would speak who answered those who already knew him. Recognition is anticipated on account of old acquaintance renewed. A query then comes as to whether the new arrival wants to be included in this field of action and society. This attitude of free choice is characteristic of the whole Rite really, but is particularly emphasised here. No one will ever be forced into this kind of a Circle, but on the other hand no unwelcome intruders are likely to gain entrance in the first place. The keynote of this entire association is "compatible companionship". Therefore membership is a matter of mutuality which has to be recognised at the entrance.

For the first time in this round the wayfarer is asked to identify other individuals. Does he in fact appreciate who or what they amount to before being allowed into closer contact. The old question, "who do you say that I am?" is very much more than an idle enquiry. How far do most humans really know or understand the true worth or otherwise of others? Here is the blunt challenge of, "What do I (or we) mean to you?" and an accurate estimation of opinion is expected. No flowery or flattering descriptions. Just a basic belief of how these humans actually appear in the eyes or heart of someone approaching them. Out of such an understanding, it is possible to build up a genuine and solid relationship. One intentionally false note here would invalidate everything. Any society accepting false terms of association is bound to fall apart if the slightest external pressures are applied. Get relationships right to start with, and the rest will work itself out. That is how matters are meant to begin here—on the right footing. Traditionally, the right foot should cross the entrance first, as a sign that entrants mean to behave well during their stay, and this old custom is worth observing when the moment comes.

*"Come in and be
At home with we."*

Now the would-be entrant identifies those already within the Field or whoever will be included in it as his friends and family. The closest possible contacts humans can have among each other. Those who may be loved, trusted, respected, and relied on in all possible conditions or circumstances of Life. Others who may be lived with intimately and, if possible, infinitely. People between whom there need be no concealment of consciousness because they live together on the same levels of Inner life. Those who belong to each other by their rights of birth and Blood. This has nothing to do with so called social or "class" structures met with on Earth whatever. These are usually rather poor imitations of Inner actualities. The family and blood groupings here are strictly those arising out of spiritual associations and linkages which have formed over a very far line of Life indeed. Each individual member of such families only belongs thereto because that particular position has been duly and truly earned by Life experience and effort. The Blood-grouping is an internal affair of "Cosmic chemistry", for which there is no commercial substitute available on Earth. To "belong with the Blood" here, means to deserve such close connection with those who have "gained the Grail".

However, entrance into these Circles is not exactly an entirely easy affair. The initial interrogation goes on to enquire what the entrant brings with him to be shared by everyone else. The reply, "Another as we will," means that the individual intends to increase or enhance the whole collective consciousness by the amount of awareness he holds in himself. His abilities, skills, qualities, in fact his whole natural range of personal potentials is being offered freely for acceptance by the one will which binds these beings together. In doing so, the individual identifies his own will with that held in common among this community.

Still he is asked for some guarantee of good faith. In reply, he assures his questioner that to the best of his belief he shares the same fundamental Faith in Life as all others present or in communion with the Circle. As a pledge, he produces a token which is examined, altered, and dealt with. Divinity is thanked in the accepted sense of representation. Even now, there has to be a final check on the character and intentions of the individual seeking entry. At the same time that being has a right to an assurance of good faith and treatment from all others. This mutual compact with consciousness is symbolised by the Shield, which signifies a promise of peace and friendship among the fellowship in this Field.

The "pledge around its edge" is the Golden Rule of Life arranged in metrical shape for the sake of ritual impact and remembrance. In point of fact, this particular arrangement seems extremely effective and apposite. It implies a relationship not only between those of blood-ties, but everyone else as well, thus inferring the possibility of a Cosmic Companionship formed among all living beings with esteem for each other. A sort of universal "Truth Treaty", or "Peace Pact" acceptable by everybody of good will everywhere. On such a condition, each entrant will be more than welcomed into whatever Circle of Life is rightfully their own. In this case, the applicant lays a right hand firmly on the Shield and makes a solemn promise to keep the same Faith with his Family and Friends which they share with him. No more can be said by anyone alive. It is possible that after this a recognition handgrip may be exchanged between entrant and examiner, or a seasonal greeting given according to custom. Then with right foot first, the newcomer rejoins old friends waiting in the Circle with a welcome.

What happens now? Whatever generally happens when old family friends get together and enjoy each other's company. Food, friendship, and fun. Conversation, information, and calculation. Any activity indulged in by people living on common levels of culture and civilisation. This is the characteristic of these Circles which distinguishes them from ordinary worldly arenas. In Earthlife, we are accustomed to all kinds of cultures and states of civilisation mixed up into a hotch-potch having really little in common except commercial and financial interests which produce a pseudo-culture chiefly for the sake of profit. This results in a dichotomy of at least two distinct culture-levels. That which people would naturally associate with because of their inherent characteristics, and another they accept because of availability or on account of its communal convenience. One we actually want, and the other we more or less have to take. The condition of civilised culture prevailing in these symbolic Circles, is ideally that which conforms with the natural spiritual standards of those contained therein. That is to say, whatever state of living we would feel essentially our own, quite apart from economic, political or any kind of pressure at all. What we should be, in fact, if absolute freedom allowed us to assume the Life-condition of our choice, and this fitted in completely with the choosings of others.

So in the Field or our Circle, people behave as they expect of each other according to conventions in force, and depending on what general codes of conduct apply. Why it should be assumed sometimes that old-time pagans practised nothing but fantastic sexual orgies in these Circles, only modern sado-masochists could answer. They had plenty of other business and social obligations to transact, and different forms of entertainment could arouse their interests and enthusiasm. Living as they did, food and security had higher priorities for them than sex. Any ex-prisoner of war or comparably placed person would confirm this. On the whole, early pagan communities were far less sex-oriented than modern ones. They were apt to take their sex in quite simple and straightforward ways, and were generally seasonal about it. Any sort of orgy as understood in Roman days or more recently, would have been far beyond the means of early Rollrighters. What sexual efforts they were capable of had to be directed into the general struggle for sheer survival and producing sufficient progeny to keep pace with their mortality rate. They did not play with sex, it was hard enough for them to work at it.

What people do outside the Circle-Field is their own affair, but their conduct inside it belongs to everyone rightfully included therein. That is the general rule of the Rollrights or any such Circles. One characteristic of those far-time farmer fighters who established the Stones should certainly be emulated nowadays. Their innate good humour and delight in laughter. They were always ready to smile at the slightest suitable stimulus. Such simple things could make them so wonderfully happy. It took so little to please them in terms of our present values. What is the price of pleasure now as compared with then? To recapture something of the Rollright spirit, the entertainment enjoyed in the Circle-Field ought to depend on people making their own gaiety among themselves rather than relying on radios, recordings, portable television, or any kind of commercially provided pleasure. Circle companionship should be something coming out of folk from inside themselves, and not pushed into them for the sake of profit.

There surely ought to be singing and dancing of some description. Nobody should have to be told how to arrange this activity. Though the "Rollright Song" previously given does not strictly belong entirely with the Ritual script, it, or something like it, makes a very good inclusion. Its wording needs no explanation, except perhaps the line mentioning "flags, fodder, flax, and frig." This is a very old saying to signify the four basics once considered necessary for making mankind happy. "Flags" meant the stones of a shelter or house. The Stones of a Circle, too. "Fodder", of course, is food. "Flax" means clothing, and the best material made of linen. "Frig" had no salacious significance whatsoever originally. It indicated simply human love-relationships between men and women in their homes. The goddess Frigga, from which the word derives, was patroness of connubial bliss, family love, good housewives, and faithful marriage partners. She even invited happily married people on Earth to come and live in her luxury home after they died, so that they need never part. Frigga typified the ideal woman of every man. Any dirt attached to the word only reflects unpleasantness in the minds of those denigrating a loving home-life between humans. The sum total of this old saw therefore means that if a man had a good stone house, fine food, splendid clothes, and a wonderful wife, what more might he possibly want on Earth, or even in Heaven? These were the "Four Blessings" hoped for in old time, and invoked upon friends. Why should we wish anything less worthy now?

At the conclusion of the Circle convention, clues are given in the valediction about the one-time activities which took place there, and might well be equated yet. To keep faith together and hold a feast. It was expected that everyone coming to the feast would bring some contribution for the pot. The rich brought much in the way of meat, while the poor might have only brought a few herbs or some firewood. In the end, everyone had put something into the feast and taken something out of it, so that the meal could be considered as communal. It had to be shared in love and trust, because nothing would have been easier than to poison everyone with a few fatal ingredients in a pot all ate and drank from together. This was what "witch-work" meant then, and why such "workers of wickedness" were so feared and hated. Only those with complete faith in each other's integrity dared eat communally and enjoy their meal in comfort.

Sharpening swords on Stones was once literally practised, though of course not in the very early days. As short bronze daggers came into use, it was often done to give the edge a rub or so on the "family Stone" in the hope of bringing favours from ancestral spirits in battle. It was also a sort of promise to fight for the same Tradition or inherited benefits therefrom. To upraise a Rod, staff, or spear, was much like planting a flagstaff in later days. It signified, "Here I am, now what does everyone else want to do about it." A friendly or fierce gesture depending entirely upon how it was done, and what the staff in question stood for. Each staff represented its owner, and here they were raised in friendship.

To drink a loving-cup together is a custom happily with us yet, whether to honour the highest concept of Divinity, or cement a purely human companionship. No spiritual or social Rite would be complete without it, and this is both. The cup need not be particularly alcoholic. A cup of tea or other welcome fluid may be just as valuable if accepted in the right spirit. A cup of plain water given generously is a far finer spiritual symbol than the richest liqueur offered grudgingly or superficially.

"Praising the Old Ones" not only means speaking well of ancient Concepts which have stood by us in the past, but also remembering and honouring the debts we owe to our human ancestry. We ourselves are those "Old Ones" of our times who are the ancestors our descendants may or may not praise, depending on their opinions of us. If we value their opinions at all, then it is only fair that we should think well of whoever we consider ourselves worthy descendants of. It is a good thing to link ourselves in with a line of Life reaching each side of our present positions. Even though we have no conscious knowledge of who our ancestors were, it extends Inner awareness to go in search of them on deep levels. That is why people attached so much importance to "tables of genealogy" or "ancestral tablets". Those provided a "clearway of consciousness" along which Inner time travel became possible. Hence one great significance of Tradition.

Keeping the promise of the Shield is always a cause for congratulation in any Circle. There is an unspoken implication here that peace prevailed because only a Shield-selected company were allowed into the Field. The saying of words refers partly to the passwords or recognition signals given, and partly to a right choice of conversation while in company together. To try anyone's will means to discover their intentions and also to find out one's own true Will in regard to Life. Making a pledge or a promise is to put up spiritual security for future contingencies. Providing this comes within limits of commonsense, it does help to guide intentions along lines to be followed later. Quite apart from any ritual pledging, ordinary private promises between people come into this category. No promise should be made to other Circle members unless there is the firmest intention of fulfilling it if humanly possible. There is no room at all for half-hearted or politely unmeant promissory phrases in this Field. Whatever is said must be honestly intended, so that the reputation of the Circle for reliability is never doubted.

Tying true knots goes back to the times where "Knot-knowledge" might mean the difference between life and death. It still does for mountaineers, and others whose lives hang literally from threads. Tying "Magical knots" means to take a stream of consciousness or a train of thought as if it were a cord, then manoeuvre it around as though knotting it into some specific tie. The result is a kind of nodal complex around that particular point which may serve a number of various purposes. Binding and loosing the "fatal cords" connecting us with Life was, and still is, one of the arcane arts.

The "calling of Names" means more than invoking Divine Images by their descriptive titles. It means identifying by name or recognising the different types of Inner energy worked with, and the calling forth

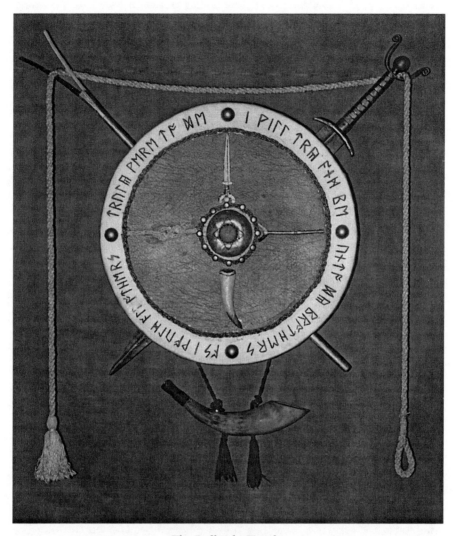

The Rollright Trophy

The "Rollright Trophy" is an association of the major Magical Symbols in the Western Tradition. These are the Rod, Sword, Shield, Cup and Cord.

Here the Shield is shown centrally with its "peace-pledge" inscribed in runes. The metal boss holds a single naturally spherical stone meaning "harmony". The Sword is of the "Halstadt" pattern, circa 1500 BC. The Rod is bifurcated to show that life is best ruled by making a central choice between opposite alternatives. The Cup is of the old Horn type which could be blown from one end or quaffed from the other, indicating output and input of life. The Cord has a male (tasselled) and female (looped) end. All sorts of significant designs are possible with this.

Altogether this "trophy" contains in itself most of the vital keys to both ancient and modern occidental occultism.

of these energies among those present. It may also refer to the custom of bestowing new names on individuals initiated into the Circle. Every Stone had its own special "Name", and initiates were once supposed to know and call them all in turn. Striking the Stones is a way of "calling forth" their Inner contacts with individuals or families. For instance, if a member of the Circle were Absent, to "strike his Stone" was supposed to make contact with him via the collective consciousness concerned. The same went for discarnate members. To "send out a summons", the appropriate Stone had to be struck with the right signal of knocks. Then again, to strike the Stones meant making artifacts, or sparks for lighting fires. Striking a bargain was once worked by the people concerned smiting a hand down on some sacred Stone to seal the transaction. If both or all parties struck the Stone with their hands together, the deal was completed. Stone-striking has a great deal of meaning with a Circle.

Love and Life obviously go together, but who knows what the elusive quality of "Luck" is? Entirely apart from its vague connotation of a somewhat unfair bias by Fate on behalf of an undeserving favourite, the term derives from "lucis" or "Lux", the Power of Light. By linking Love, Life, and Light, the triple invocation of Divine Beneficence is made. "Good luck" wished anyone is another version of, "May the God of Light be with you." That is to say, may Illumination be granted, and deliverance from evil assured. If this commonplace phrase is accompanied by consciously directed intentions with correct interpretation of its meaning, it will be all the more effective.

Blowing the Horn around the Stone has already been dealt with, but it is also a euphemism for going round the Circle while "blowing the horn", or exchanging cheerful greetings and conversation with others. It is like "circulating" round a large party or convention, so that many contacts are made, and new friends met with. There are two main uses for a horn in this respect. It may be blown (or spoken through) to establish communication with others, but it should then be reversed and placed to the ear in order to hear what they say in reply. In other words, people should get in touch with each other all round the Circle and exchange ideas. There was once an old way of getting together with a pair of horns so that each person spoke close into the large end of a horn with its small end held to the other person's ear. This was a very secret way of speaking, and became part of the "mouth to ear" Tradition of "Inner teaching".

Lighting a fire with "wind and wit" once called for a firemaker's very special skill, and was considered a high operation of Magic. So it was then.

The Fire became the centre point of the Circle around which everyone gathered, and a Circle without Fire would be only a body without a Life. Wind and wit signify inspiration and wisdom. So does Light come into our lives, and that is what these Circles are all about. A Fire lit rightly with "wind and wit" is capable of passing those qualities along to other fires kindled from it elsewhere. Sometimes glowing embers from the Circle Fire were taken home in clay fire-pots wherein they might be kept smouldering for a long while by judicious addition of fuel on the way. Thus everyone's home fire could be kindled from one and the same source as a memorial of happy meetings. It is essential to have a practical fire of some sort even as a spirit stove for brewing tea within the Circle. A Circle meeting without a Fire is unthinkable. Many forms are possible now, from a struck match to a pressure-gas device. Traditionally, a sacred Fire should be kindled with flint, and a modern spark-struck lighter fulfils this specification quite reasonably.

The custom of taking embers home to light personal fires with had considerable mystical meaning. One little-realised function of these Stone Circles was to act as a residual storage place for ancestral memories which would "spark off" genetic chains of consciousness reaching back into past incarnations of initiates. Say, for instance, someone entered among the Stones for the first occasion in that incarnation. If they were truly a member of the Circle in the sense of belonging to it before, then this contact would almost automatically awaken the deep consciousness leading back to that past point and beyond. It might also reflect as far into the future. So long as the Stones stood, they could act as agents for arousing these finer Inner faculties of whoever belonged with the families connected thereto. In that sense, the "embers" left over from a previous incarnation could relight the Fire of Inner Illumination revealing the reasons behind the present one. So far might the principles behind the Magical element of Fire extend, and farther yet until Eternity.

There is now nothing left to do in the Circle Field except give thanks to Hu in the presence of all, and wish a welfaring to everyone. Having come together in the happiest of companies, everybody has to go back Earthwards individually with hope in his heart and pleasing memories in his mind. Memories are difficult or inadvisable to raise sometimes, but hope should be a constant companion of Life at all levels. One custom to be observed here is that of never looking back in the direction of the Circle once it is quitted. The way back is only to be properly found by going forward until the Life-course curves through Cosmos enough to complete the return circuit. That is the correct procedure.

When the parting point of the complex is reached, the Tomb has become a Womb, our only way of reaching incarnate embodiment again. The Symbol here is the Cord of Truth which provides us with clues for knowing what to look for in Life. Equipped with one of these, we can follow Fate anywhere. Again a challenge is heard, and now the admission is made that the individual intends to travel in search of Truth, yet knows not the Way thereto. What human does? If we did, we should not still be here hunting for it.

A play on words about Knot and Nil is made. The Cord is shown as a noose (circle of Zero), gradually closing down to Nothing and then pulling out of itself entirely to take any design chosen by the manipulator. This is to illustrate how we should make what we will out of what is "Nothing" to everyone else. So should we learn the truly Magical art of making our lives as we go along out of the Infinity behind us. Given a "cord of consciousness" connecting us with the deepest Truth of our origination, there is no reason why this should not be so. Therefore birthseekers are advised to keep this Inner contact by tying themselves to Life with the Cord linking back to their spiritual sources. This actually leads through whatever especial esoteric Tradition is theirs because of Initiation or other associations connected with their natural "Faith-families". Though the Rollrights are established on what is fundamentally a universal pattern, they do link up with what has come to be recognised as the "Western Tradition." Something much more mysterious and elusive than any Oriental system of Inner life. It is indigenous to "natives" of a certain Cosmic Life-category, regardless of their physical residence on this planet. As they go into incarnation, they take with them an instinctive feeling of where and with whom they rightly belong as evolving living entities. Here the Cord, or "line of descent" becomes their Symbol of remembrance and recognition regarding the Tradition it represents.

Here follows another "Earthbirth" mime representing re-entry into incarnation. It will be noticed that no "Token" passes here. This is because we are supposed to incarnate in order to obtain the necessary tokens for earning our way back. We start our incarnations with a cord for collecting our Life-tokens by "noosing them with knowledge". That should be sufficient. In actuality, it is only necessary to kneel briefly here for the reading of the Rite, or symbolise emergence upon Earth by some easy action such as crouching in a womb-posture, then rising into an upright position with upraised and out-stretched arms as if embracing a whole life time of existence.

"Take this Cord and tie Yourself to Life for aye."

There is a point to be noted here also that "Good" and "God" are identified in the phrase "Good be with you (Hu)". Then the natural response follows, "And with you (Hu), too". Both reader and respondent are saluting the Divine Principle in each other. If everyone alive were able to recognise this same Spirit in everybody else, the whole of Life would alter into a very different condition than it has deviated into here at present. So may it yet be restored.

Lastly, the re-entrant into ordinary dimensions of natural Life on this Earth gives the Greeting-call of self-relationship toward all else that IS, or maybe Might Be in being. To Mother Earth and Father Sky. This world, the entire Universe and everyone in it. The Spirit of Life as a Cosmos of Comprehension, yet conscious of and as each individual life within It. Then the challenge of every single living soul to Life however it comes, "HERE COME I! " The "Cry of Creation" reputed to have begun life at the very commencement of Cosmos. Living is acclaimed as a coming, a constant arrival, a continuance of change, and Infinite immanence, a becoming into being. Life is a continual coming around a Cosmic Circle of Consciousness. HERE COME I may be interpreted as the cry of every infant as it appears from the womb, or the Call addressed to Life in the Otherworld as we leave this one. We do not *go* to any kind of "afterlife", we *come* thereto. Thinking this way puts us in the right direction round our Life-courses.

Even though all this covers the general outline of the Rollright Ritual script, it has only scraped the surface enough to show what lies beneath for the benefit of those seeking even deeper spiritual solidities. Once the Inner Gates guarded by the Stones opens up for everyone, there is endless exploration to be encountered ahead. According to the old legend about them, the Stones were really men who had gone to sleep in that form, and when the time came they would wake up and continue living. All they needed was the "Magic Word" spoken among them to accomplish this awakening. Can this at last be possible? Only those who work the Will within the Words will ever know for sure.

CHAPTER EIGHT

THE RIGHTS OF THE RITE

There is no question or even a suggestion that the Rollright Ritual dealt with here is identical in form with any used in olden days at this site. It is an Inner evolution of the same fundamentals which have always been employed by Mankind one way or another for establishing relationships with Infinite Identity. What links the Ritual especially with the Rollright Stone system is its pattern, which follows the formula on which such stone complexes seem to have been constructed.

As humanity grew old enough to appreciate something of the Greater Universe around this little planet and our wider Cosmic environs, the Stone Circles became much more complicated affairs altogether. Stones in some stood for solar, lunar, and stellar arrangements, or the principles by which whole nations of people came into combination together. Despite all the intricacies and impressiveness of Stonehenge or anywhere else, however, we should not forget those first forefathers (and mothers!) crouching in Circles round a "forefire". By the time Circles like Stonehenge were raised with careful calculations and well-organised labour, humans had already forgotten or dismissed as out of date many of their primitive practices. In its day, Stonehenge was an ultra modern improvement upon an ancient social structure. More distantly in Egypt then, people were praising the scientific and engineering advances which had made the Pyramids possible. How immeasurably superior these seemed then as compared with the pathetic heaps of common stones placed by ancestors over graves to stop wild animals digging up dead relatives for food. Modern Man has always regarded his forebears with pitying patronage or some sense of superiority.

If humans live long enough individually or collectively, they are bound to notice the "Cosmic curvature" of Time which seems to bring the past back to them with ever increasing importance. Old people seldom remember much of what has happened the day before, but long forgotten incidents of childhood return with startling clarity and significance. The same principle applies with people as a whole over far longer periods of time. In this world, we are more concerned now with what happened some thousands of years ago than we were a few hundred years back. But are we really "looking back", or are we actually *looking forward* into our past from a higher level of Life? Does our increasing interest in the past indicate greater concern for our future? It undoubtedly does.

Consider a newly born baby. Has such a person any past? Yes. Very much so indeed. The entire past of every single ancestor imprinted into the genes. This quite apart from any spiritual genetics imparted from former individual incarnations. In fact, its past is a baby's only hope of having a future at all. Yet we do not (or should not) *return* to the past, but *advance* to it through the present. As the Rite says, "HERE COME I". The Rollright Pattern keeps bringing us *forward* around its cyclic course so that we should keep covering the same Cosmos with ever evolving comprehension.

In this Rollright Ritual, therefore, we are not going back to any kind of past practise, but progressing forward to further extensions of these points into the immeasurable future. Regression means reversal of a Life-process, with the implication of this being an intentional act against the course of Cosmos. This was one reason why anti-Cosmic, or leftward circling was taken to be symbolic of deliberate evil or defiance of Divinity. Only the intention made this so, of course, because a Circle or spiral is both *pro* and *contra*-clockwise depending from which side it is observed.

Real regression is only possible by the destructive dispersal of all advances of awareness made between any present point and whatever period in the past represents the degree of regression reached. For example, it would be *regression* to smash up and reduce to wreckage the machinery of any present period, but *progression* to supersede it, so that better work of the same class can be done without it at all. After that, the work itself may be superseded so that our lives are much happier and finer when effort evolves into enjoyment. Therefore, this Ritual is not intended as a revival of primitive practices or a reversion towards less cultured customs than those passing for civilised procedures today. To the contrary. It projects the present state of the past into future extensions of Inner existence. Nor is the Rite supposed to be anything in the way of "neo-paganism", or "fragments of a forgotten Faith", or whatever might suggest the recrudescence of some specific bygone religion. It stands, as the Stones themselves have always stood, for an expression of Man's inherent instinct to relate himself with Infinite Identity. This same spiritual quality which has accompanied us unbrokenly along the whole line of our lives from a commencement of Cosmos until now, and who knows toward what Ultimate?

There is but One Faith for Mankind to follow. It may be presented in as many different ways as there are humans alive, or by a lesser number of distinctive formations related to eras, collections of scriptures, Founder-figures, or any other formation factor. Fundamentally, it is One, and its variations are due to interpretations arising from the complexities of human consciousness trying to cope with concepts somewhat beyond the range of normal comprehension. It is true that many little simplicities make a mass of complexity but sooner or later all those complexities are sure to straighten out into a Supreme Simplicity. So may it be with the Faith of Life muddled up by Man despite the best of his intentions.

In early Stone Circle times, people did not distinguish their Life-Faith by any special title or categorical description. Religion in the sense we see it nowadays had no particular meaning. It was taken for granted people would relate themselves with Whatever was There however came most naturally to them, and on the whole there was an overall kind of general pattern most of Mankind appeared to recognise in common.

When migrant Man began to settle in definite areas long enough to establish local Life-roots in some particular vicinity, societies became stabilised around specific systems associated with individual communities. So commenced divergencies of customs and distinctions which eventually led to hostile differences of organised opinions. Underneath everything the whole while, however, lay the same Primal Pattern. The more Mankind digressed from it and messed up its meaning, the more quarrelsome and divided among each other people grew. And still grow. If we go forward far enough for the past to reappear as it should in the future, most of us might arrive at some common conclusions in the same Circle, and that would make for very cheerful companionship all round.

As in early times, there is no need for any specifically nominated religious System to establish a world-wide domination of beliefs on organised lines like a spiritual supermarket chain. All Mankind must be free to find a Life-Faith each for him or herself. Where Circles of agreement come together for fulfilment of this Faith by mutually accepted methods, then let such Will be worked therein, but let it never be inflicted elsewhere unwillingly. That is how trouble begins, by unwarranted interference with the accepted arrangements of any Circle's internal affairs. Once we learn how to live in correct Circle-relationships among ourselves and with Cosmos, there will be far greater hope of a happy and harmonious humanity in our temporary home in this Earth.

Had a hypothetical time-traveller met up with a Rollrighter or anyone else in that era and demanded to know what that person's religious beliefs were, the Circler would have had a hard job to understand the question, and the querent an equally difficult problem to follow the reply. Both would have lacked an adequate symbology in common unless they were qualified initiates of an inter-related Inner association of ideologies. The Rollrighter would have made it plain that what he believed was something like what most of the others believed in their Circles. Like their High God, Whoever That was, nobody knew a Name or ever would. Nobody spoke about That normally, but sometimes people said "He" or "She". If "religion" meant a lot of rules about what to think and do about this "Who knows Hu"—well, this was something that just worked out as one went along. If people came together in a Circle, that kind of thing sort of came out of them from inside. Some Circles did this and others did that. That was the way things had to be. There was no special name for what any Circle decided among themselves. Why should there be? Life was Life.

That was it. The Life-members of every Circle got together and arrived at common beliefs through interchanges of their conscious energies guided by Inner Intelligence. Whether they were relatively right or wrong is beside the point. What matters is that they were sincerely trying to reach toward Ultimate Truth by their own efforts at spiritual evolution. Clumsy and crude as their attempts may seem to us now, those were no more awkward or ineffectual than our own conveniently forgotten misbehaviours during childhood.

Though these early people gave their Faith no generic title, some who abandoned Circles for various reasons and chose to live otherwise, invented terms of disparagement for what they had forsaken. A late form of one such term was "pagan", signifying "countryman", or "peasant". Later still "heathen" or "heath-dweller", implying a crude, backward, uncultured, and savage sort of creature. All slightingly contemptuous references to earlier and Earthier attempts at civilisation. Why? What was so wonderful about the "modernism" of its time which made Stone Circling so out of date and obsolete that contempt was the only form of consideration it deserved from the "permissives" of that period?

The answer is simple. Inside Circles, anti-social human qualities such as dishonesty, ill-will, deception, injustice, and other unpleasant characteristics, are easy to notice and relatively simple to deal with. Someone does a dirty and deceitful trick on another member of the same society. What happens? The "do-badder" is either executed or expelled. Nobody else wants to deal with that person locally. So he is "excommunicated" from that particular Circle. This happens all over the world. Thousands of expelled or unwelcome humans set up their own type of society in opposition to the old Circles, and "cities of the plains" rose everywhere to outmode the one-time "high places".

What was the advantage of quitting those Circles in the first place? Plenty, for those with no spiritual or social scruples. Outside the Circles, they could build up a type of civilisation wherein it was not only practical but also most profitable to lie, cheat, steal, murder, and generally take every unfair advantage of other simpler minded humans with comparative impunity. Inside a Circle, crime was far more detectable and punishable than in looser limits outside. It was easier to work evil in uncycled chaotic communities than in circular Cosmic ones. Especially if an atmosphere of acceptance toward such evils could be artificially created. Once the general exodus from the Circles started for the sake of greed-gratifications, it became impossible to keep them together in anything like the same Spirit they were originally intended to stand for. So far as "modernising" Mankind was concerned, Circles were "Out", and cities were "In".

There followed a long, long time in which simplicity or straight-forwardness became sneeringly associated with stupidity, and crooked cunning admired as cleverness. The sharps of the cities ran their kind of rings round the flats coming from the Circles. Have we yet entirely evolved out of that epoch? Eventually the old companionship of the Circles grew more and more tenuous until it sank into semi-secrecy, though never into irrevocable oblivion. The Spirit of the silent Stones may seem somnolent, but it has never slept to a point past all awakening. In fact, it is quietly arising in this present period. Those once silenced Stones are beginning to speak again.

A possibility exists of the Edenic myths being at least partially connected with very early Circle-dwelling days. Race memories may have handed down idealised impressions of times gone by when people lived happily in Circles because they knew and trusted each other among small family groups. There was a spirit of unison among them which seemed like God. Eventually, however, dishonesty and sex quarrels broke up the sanctity of the Circles, and humans were expelled into the world outside where murder and unchecked social evils abounded. Ever since then, a deep conviction has remained with many members of the human race that if only the principles of Circle-Life on both local and world-wide scales could ever be re-established, everyone might be happy and harmonious once more. Who knows? Perhaps there is a chance of this happening yet.

Life, on Earth at any rate, has to be formulated on all its levels. The Rollright Ritual is a formula for the Faith in Life which binds Man's most basic beliefs to the bed-rock of his reasons for being on this planet in the first instance. It also leads us up to our ultimate take-off, for we certainly cannot stay here forever. Once, Baby wanted the Moon, now Baby is actually playing with it. Soon spoiled brat may be breaking his toys again. Yet there will come a time when we outgrow Cosmic childhood and become fit people to take our places at the grown-up Round Tables of the galaxies. This could even be because we once managed to set out crude images of their Patterns in stone down here on our nursery floor, and have been following roughly along the ideas ever since.

The Rollright ritual is not representative of any one limited orthodox religion, despite its sacramental symbolism of a bread-wine Faith-feast. If anything, it holds traces of the oldest Mysteries celebrated among Mankind, though at the same time it is positively pointed toward the youngest kind of "Mystique" reincarnating again through the now rising generations. They may bring Faith with them as usual, but once more a Faith without a Name anyone feels much like defining. Why so? Mostly because once we attach a name to anything it becomes limited accordingly, and necessarily excludes whatever we believe it is not. Not in actuality, of course, but in our consciousness of it. Furthermore, we have to do this in order to live within bounds of reason and intelligence. Except at one point. The primal point of all where our first definable concepts appear from the Zero of infinite Inconceivability. There has to be this "Fount of Faith" from which everything we shall ever think about and all the words we shall ever use come forth among us. This is our original or "Old" Life-Faith, for which there cannot be a name that any words of ours are capable of containing. The Symbol of such a Zero, of course, is a Circle. A Stone Circle. The Old Original form of our earliest Faith which we are even now re-approaching for the sake of survival again.

Probably every young generation since civilisation began has been condemned by its elders as immoral, idle, indifferent and irreligious. Apart from individuals actually deserving such descriptions, the majority of young men and women on Earth are always looking for a Life-Faith which never seems present in their own parents. So, if they have any sense, they will claim to have found it exclusively, supposing themselves in the right and everybody else in the wrong. If they have supersense, they will find their forms of Life-Faith, and leave others the same freedom in separate Circles. It should not take long for everyone to realise that all such Circles become automatically included in a Cosmos containing every Life-Circle existing. Young folk may suppose they are looking for a "new" Faith, or Way of Life, but they are really seeking the Oldest

Faith-Origin of all. Providing they name it not as any ism, schism, anity, or insanity, and recognise a Primal Power they realise is beyond their determination, though within their ability to approach otherwise, they might find something of what they look for in Life.

Once conscious contact with a fundamental Life-Faith is made, there is no reason whatever why people should not continue living in whatever Circles of convenience suit their especial spiritual requirements closest. Herein Deities may be identified and named according to need, religious rules observed, and all the rest of human holy habits honoured. There is nothing to prevent people from being most conscientious Christians, Jews, Buddhists, or following any spiritual system while at the same time being believers in a Life-Faith quite beyond the limits of this planet or Solar System. So deep it cannot be declared, so profound it may not be proclaimed, so normal it needs no name, yet so close to Consciousness that it cannot be conceived as anything to be aware of. Something we do not think or talk about, because it actually *is* that awareness in ourselves which does the thinking and talking about everything and everyone else. This is the Faith which the Rollright formula seeks to find symbolically.

Though the practical performance of the Ritual will only prove valuable for those able to work it properly, there should be no doubt that there is a very real and deep-seated need for the principles of Life connected with our old Stone Circles in these modern times. We have not outgrown them yet, or for that matter become big enough to claim our proper places in their Cosmic counterparts. Anyone apt to doubt this, ought to consider the amazing increase of visitors to, and interest in, these ancient Stone sites. It is startling how many people in this age of mechanical miracles and stupendous Space achievements are going out of their way in order to stand and stare at plain Stones. To watch their behaviour for any length of time can be quite fascinating, and to record some of their conversations and comments extremely amusing. Few, if any, will admit a specially spiritual reason for coming, yet come they do in ever larger numbers. Why?

What makes such an influx of modern visitors to the Stones especially interesting is that they are mostly just ordinary average people. Not student-specialists in particular of anything like archaeology, anthropology, prehistory, or the like. Simply the same sort of individual who used to operate these Circles when they were in working order. They probably *are* the same folk nostalgically attracted by something they instinctively realise protected them from perils and promoted their best interests in the past. Their unspoken hope, of course, is that maybe the Circles might have the same meaning for the future. Which they do indeed, if we are able to re-construct them not so much out of Stone, but with the Spirit those Stones have always stood for.

The chances are that only the merest minority of moderns who visit Stones of any sort would actually take an active part in the Ritual dealt with here. Almost all, however, would quite cheerfully attend any form of entertainment such as music, dancing, or feeding, which happened to be available in the Circle part of the complex. So it was in the olden days. Few came for what we would consider devotional purposes in comparison with the multitudes who turned up for social and commercial contacts. Seldom did people do the full round of the 'Rights, except on solemn occasions when everybody felt constrained to make the circuit. Mostly they came for the fun and games in the Circle and the opportunity of a bargain there maybe. That was about their limit in the way of religious observance. Just like people today.

Lack of liturgical ability does not indicate atheistic or anti-social tendencies. It means no more than a natural incapacity for relating with the Life-Spirit above certain cultural levels. There comes a point in all people where they run out of words and can find no adequate actions to participate in the intellectual or active content of what Life presents to them. Yet they are still able to feel and appreciate its impact on themselves. Many people would silently witness this Ritual worked by others without attempting to participate themselves, then afterwards join in heartily with the social celebrations. Once they enter a familiar field they get going with the rest. This is quite an average expectation of behaviour among ordinary Circle visitors to any ceremonial gathering likely to be celebrated there or in simulated surroundings. It would seem best that even such a simple devotional ceremony as the Rollright Ritual should be restricted to private practice among full participants. Nor would it be really wise to produce it as a spectacle. Spectators seldom contribute anything of very great spiritual value toward a scene of Inner action meaning no more to them than uncertain entertainment.

For participation on all general levels of living activity at a single occasion, the Stations of the Rollrights could comfortably be adapted to four quite separate forms of human behaviour. The first and last point would obviously be a "sorting out" place where procedures were explained, events outlined, welcomes extended, programmes or pamphlets offered and so forth. A kind of "public relations" office as it were, with facilities for making introductions, and offering quite a range of specialised services. The next Station of the King Stone would be a lecture place and Forum. A type of "Intelligence Exchange". All sorts of related talks and discussions might be given and taken here. At the Counsellors or "Whispering Knights", of course, only devotional and spiritual exercises or purely meditational periods would be permitted. Over in the Circle entertainments and eating going on all the while. It should be a reasonable expectation that the noise level of the Circle would not seriously interfere with other activities.

A day spent visiting a "Rollright Convention" of this nature would undoubtedly prove most rewarding. Pilgrims could pick and choose their points of participation as they felt inclined, and so there would be something for everyone, just as there was originally. A real "Feast of Faith". No need to hold it on the actual site of the Stones at all, because the pattern is of primary importance much more than the place. What would constitute the convention of a Rollright Faith-focus, is the combination of those four categorical activities of human consciousness into a complete complex. The whole round would call out the qualities of Sincerity, Sagacity, Spirituality, and Sociability from people in that order. Perhaps relating these together might be the single factor of Simplicity. Surely it could scarcely be possible for anyone to exert themselves in such a manner for a whole day and not become somewhat better for the effort?

It is a recognised property of human nature that when we feel ourselves endangered or overstressed we automatically reach as far back toward our roots as we can for supports or an escape route. Official atheists will invoke God instinctively if an unexpected crisis comes. Strong men sob pathetically for their mothers as death approaches. Reactions vary over a very wide range depending on individuals, but the principle of reaching rootwards is the same in the case of single souls or an entire nation. Humans know without being told in so many words that their only real hopes of survival are bound up with the basics or roots of their beings. A sense of being "uprooted", or without any solid spiritual support anywhere is about the most hopeless feeling in this world. That is exactly what young people in particular find so frightening in their dealings with modern Mankind.

Social, financial, political, or similar insecurities in this world are difficult but not impossible to cope with, providing, and entirely depending upon, that there is a sense of confident spiritual security which transcends temporal uncertainties and dubieties. Given sufficient spiritual strength arising from this Inner identification with a Cosmic condition of consciousness, and Life becomes a possibility of progress beyond Earthly existence no matter what troubles turn up. Without this one vital factor, however, humans feel helpless because they realise they have become rootless, and unless they can connect themselves back to a Life-basis somewhere or somehow, they will die out eventually altogether. That is the exact problem so many face nowadays, and why they either drift aimlessly toward an extinction which appears inevitable, or panic violently around doing this, that, and the other thing out of sheer desperation. Their pressing need for root-contacts with Inner realities is a pathetic and sorrowful affair altogether. The worst of it is that none can really help them except themselves in the last analysis. To try and force them into Faith-formulae they are unable to use would be utterly pointless and stupid. The Law of Life is that we must establish our own roots in Inner Realities of Existence by our own attempts at awareness therewith. Insofar as any creed or code offers facilities for reaching root-realisations, it helps humanity. Otherwise it is only ornamental or possibly worse.

It is this desperate necessity for finding satisfactory Life-roots which drives so many people into odd corners of consciousness looking for clues. Pseudo-paganism, what now passes for "witchcraft" (see Appendix), and almost anything appearing as if it came from some ancient stock is hastily grasped and frequently dropped in disappointment. Strange that nothing seems to horrify these moderns so much as modernity and its unsatisfying state of pseudo-spirituality. This is scarcely surprising. These are living people who cry to Cosmos for an assurance of their lives. They do not want a dead, sterile, senseless, or otherwise futile form of Divinity. They ask for Life, Fertility, Awareness, Individuality, and above all a Meaning through which they may relate themselves with what cannot be less than Eternal Entity. Either they reach these roots of themselves or they fade out from sheer lack of Life. No wonder their conduct might seem odd to less concerned or unsympathetic members of human society.

A long time ago, there were many ways of finding Liferoots which have been either cut off or seriously impeded by modern "methodologies", and until channels can be cleared again, there are bound to be many difficulties ahead. For instance, one way of Inner rooting was by race, another by family, and another by blood. Never have these root loyalties been more shaken than now. Roots might be reached through customs, creeds, beliefs, or Traditions which have now been broken, discredited, deserted, and rendered redundant, even where they are still perfectly sound, so far as utility is concerned. Then again music was another "root-reacher" if it led down deeply enough. Where has it deliberately been diverted to now, other than the profit side of various balance-sheets? What with all these and many more severances from the natural Inner rootings of humanity, who is able to say with any great degree of conscious certainty, "This is what I am, that is how I belong, and here is what I truly believe in as a Living entity."

The Rollright Ritual is a root-reacher for those who realise how to handle it like the "instrument of intention" it amounts to. In the right hands, this Ritual may be the means for many others to find that Faith in Life and the Spirit thereof which they seek so very needfully. If modern Man is losing touch with his Life-roots because old contacts are being broken off and no new ones suggested that seem suitable, there is only one thing to be done. See what an older past yet has to offer for the future. Dig more deeply into our spiritual foundations than ever before, so that the upheavals and disturbances of ephemeral events on Earth and confusions of civilisation can no longer break any of us away from our birthrights. If deep shelters have to be dug in order to survive physical destruction by nuclear energy, how much deeper yet need we go Inwardly for security against spiritual disintegration? Certainly a lot further down then we have been so recently in human history. This is not an impossible job at all. Just a very vital one to do despite any difficulties.

The spiritual specifications of a satisfactory survival project are reasonably clear. We have to ensure such a deeply positive contact with our negative sources of Inner energy that the current of living consciousness generated thereby cannot be interrupted or broken by any outside interference. To do this, we have to go down in ourselves right past any possible points of severance, until we reach an underlying Life-level of such absolute certainty that nothing the superficial happenings of our human world might produce would ever cut us off completely from that source of supply. The very worst which could occur would be a temporary demolition of our "above-ground" personal premises. Tiresome as that may be, those can always be quickly reconstructed or regrown if the substructure or roots are soundly enough set into a proper basis beneath. That is the essential prerequisite for the resurgence of Life from its immortal power-principle.

This means that in our modern world among all its urges, surges and splurges, we have to find a Life-Faith so profound and positively connected to a Cosmic nucleus of supremely negative spiritual energy that it is unshakable and utterly indestructible by anything likely to hit it at human levels. Not only can this be done, but it has already been accomplished quite quietly by many, and more loudly by some, depending on circumstances. If asked to explain, some would say by one system and others by a bewildering variety of means. A convinced

Christian, for instance, would sincerely say that faith in the Divinity of a Power personified in human form as Jesus was the entire secret. A pious Jew might claim that belief in a single Living God and adherence to the Tradition of Mosaic Law had accomplished the miracle of faith. A practising pagan could equally assert the same faith-finding through personifications of natural energies. Others would have all kinds of entirely different explanations for what is really one and the same issue—finding a basic belief in Being to belong with as a living entity.

No matter what people term themselves, or what system they adopt for the purpose, their Life-roots eventually go down to a common level from which their Faith in Life springs. No religion of any kind has exclusive rights of entrance thereto. Whoever lives may find it for themselves—if they so will, All creeds or spiritual Life-codes are of value which afford valid opportunities for reaching some degrees of identification with the realities of Inner Life. The end-effect, however, derives from the efforts of those concerned with whatever they employ for that purpose. If we want our roots we shall have to dig for them, and dig hard for a long time perhaps. This time, we shall have to reach ways to our roots which do not depend on factors of locality, nationality, social status, or anything variable by circumstances of society or civilisation. No matter where, who, what, or how we are at any given instance, we must still be able to maintain a constant contact of consciousness with our Life-Faith which will be unaffected by any alteration of ordinary living. Nothing else can give us the spiritual stability we need to stay alive and sane in a world already approaching its critical mass.

There is no point whatever in expecting to find anything of spiritual substance in the socio-commercial pseudo-culture spreading itself over the face of civilisation. This is nothing new, though its rate of acceleration seems to increase alarmingly. Those seeking real rootings of Life will have to plunge past all this commotion and penetrate deep down underneath it until a secure faith-fastening becomes possible. Then, of course, it will be spiritually quite safe to emerge again into more ordinary environments of Earthlife and associate with these to whatever extent may be essential for social survival amid entitlements we have earned through evolution. Providing we are able to keep clearways of consciousness between our rooted Inner realities and the personalised presentations of ourselves in this world, we can go on living here or anywhere else perfectly well enough for any sound purpose. It is the making of such channels and maintenance of them in good order which presents such a problem for the majority of people.

This is the whole point of working our formulae of Faith such as the Rollright Ritual. To provide something practical in the way of a symbolic experience which will result in character-changing realisations of an Inner Cosmic nature. Not only because of what has been said and done by the human participants, but additionally because of what reaches and remains with those practitioners from an Inner source of spiritual supply operating on its own account. How is this reached? Not unlike the way computer codes are automatically linked up with their appropriate contacts. Feed in the correctly coded enquiry, and it is bound to link up with all necessary points until a ne-plus-ultra totalisation results in a presentable form to its originator. Someone inserts the stimulus, the computer reacts electronically, and returns the outcome back to the stimulator.

By means of the Ritual formula, operators feed in a direct spiritual stimulus to a level of our "Collective Consciousness", where it contacts responsive points accordingly, and eventually some kind of reply should be received by the ritualist in return. It is very highly improbable this would come back as any sort of phenomena appreciable to physical senses. What can be confidently expected are realisations of changing Inner awareness in conformity with whatever the ritual practice has reacted with. These may seem so slight at first they will barely be noticeable by normal states of mind. It is rare for ritualised energy to bounce back with any severe degree of reaction almost immediately. There is very frequently quite a time-lapse by our rates or recording, between an initial input of energy into a ritual practice, and its subsequent reaction along spiritual lines. Those demanding ridiculous impossibilities from ritual work are just as much doomed to disappointments as if they had shouted a vocal demand at a computer and then kicked it violently to get a response. The only way to work rituals properly is to know the rules and follow them out faithfully.

Therefore, to operate the Rollright, or any other Ritual correctly, it must be treated fairly in the first place and no absurdities or anomalies expected of it. Providing there is a key-note of sincerity throughout, Inner responses should prove satisfactory from spiritual angles. It is not enough to merely speak the script; every word has to be lived as it is uttered in order to achieve anything worth while. There are relatively few words mainly for that reason. Better an absolute minimum of wordage with a maximum of meaning, than screeds of verbiage having only the slightest significance. Far more Inner force can be concentrated into one or two well chosen words with full consciousness focused into them, than may be dissipated by pages and pages of prose verbalised while the consciousness is concerned otherwise. With the Rollright Ritual, not a single word dare be missed or unenergised. Concentration has to be very keen and close indeed, attention being fully occupied with the meanings and implications of each phrase in turn. Though the entire script may be known by heart long previously, each occasion should be taken as if the words had never been heard before, and were opening up fresh Inner areas of awareness in order to deal with them.

This is an important point. Brief as the wording is, this is in no sense a glib Rite, every response having to be given rapidly on the heels of its query like a stage production. The Tradition behind the Rite stems from country stock, and the proverbial countryman is slow to express reactions, because his consciousness has been working deeply along perhaps a number of Inner angles before a result is obtained which satisfies his demands. He metaphorically takes the query, turns it round inside himself, plants it as deeply as he can into his connection with the collective consciousness he shares with others, then waits for the result to "come up", much as if it were a growing plant being cultivated. He is quite accustomed to living this way, and working at the normal rate of Nature.

A townsman works differently. His materials are ready-made and stock-piled. What he wants, he gets from a shelf or obtains from a shop. He buys or borrows his way around life, using what is already there or adapting available supplies into requirements. All his stuff is more or less ready to hand or comparatively convenient to obtain if money is no object. He therefore appears to produce results much more rapidly than a countryman, but in reality he is merely moving existent material about at a speed to suit his own impatience. What he does physically relates with his mental and spiritual attitudes to Life. Whatever he needs probably comes from shop-stock or some other mass-made supply. So with his thoughts and Inner ideas. These mostly come from ready-made sources. There are more of these available today than ever before, and they could be very valuable if used correctly. How many people are prepared to take some spiritual stimulus, treat it like a seed by pushing it deeply down inside themselves, then wait patiently while working with Nature for the implant to grow at its proper rate and develop in due season? That is more or less what this particular Rite is designed to do. Make Man work with Nature instead of expecting instant everything.

Therefore this is a Rite which cannot possibly be rushed. It is the thinking spaces between the words which give opportunities for the deep contacts necessary. Thought and Inner appreciation may be made as fast as Light, providing it is pushed down far enough to obtain a reaction-response from a basic spiritual level of Life, and not merely from the superficial accumulation of stock arranged on quickly available mental shelves. That is what makes this Rite so well worth doing. It practically compels its workers to go and grow fresh ideas for themselves each time so that they should have a good harvest to take home with them. This can only be gathered if sufficient co-operation with Nature along Inner lines of Life has been obtained.

A practical part of this secret is to pause briefly between each phrase of the script and its reply while the response is being Inwardly dealt with in depth. There is no need for very long or pointless pauses during which the mind wanders aimlessly from the issue. That is worse than useless. The query is bound to arise why any pause is needed if the ritual reply is already known. That is so, but the formulated reply is actually the "thought-seed" which is supposed to be planted, pondered, raised, and then reaped. The scripted reply should be known, but the responsor's reactions with it on that occasion and the Inner reply received thereby, should be worked out then and there proportionately. A slight degree of effort in the initial instance can always be expanded subsequently. What matters most is that a correct course of consciousness be initiated in the first place. Once good habits of Inner husbandry become inculcated, crops of consciousness are likely to be satisfactory.

To take an example. The entrant has to answer the query "How ask you?" He already knows the reply to be, "A leave of Life to live." Instead of instantly shooting this out without thinking about it, he silently picks up the phrase and consciously confronts it, considers it, then quite deliberately drops it as it were into his own depths carefully, intentionally consigning it to the Collective Consciousness behind him which is more capable of sorting it out and raising it up to Light than his own immediate intelligence. Confident that it will eventually come up as it should in due season, he acknowledges the whole action by confirming this much with the audibly spoken words. This indicates his readiness to accept another item in the planting program.

Be it noted that a detailed intellectual examination of each phrase as it comes during the Rite is NOT what is required. Seeds have to be planted *whole*, and not picked to pieces in a futile effort to find a little tree or whatever it is inside them. The outcome of a seed can be examined at leisure later on, after enough has grown into our dimensions to make this practical. What is needed during the Rite is a careful consideration of its presentations, as if they were fully fertilised seeds to be taken exactly as they are and dealt with as they deserve. That is to say put down to their proper depth in the right sort of Inner soil and looked after by later cultivation.

Although a deliberate intellectual dissection of these Ritual phrases is not a proper procedure during the Rite itself, there is no reason why this should not be done afterwards, even though intellect is rather a disappointing tool to use for this type of Inner investigation. Results ought never to be assessed on intellectual findings alone, for those are likely to be very limited and maybe stultifying. The really rich rewards from this Ritual are spiritual gains which are virtually impossible to define intellectually. True, there is a relationship between human intellect and a spiritual status, but this is a variable and fractional factor without an entirely fixed ratio. Insofar as intellectual examination helps to arouse interest and fix attention on the phraseology, this may be very valuable. On the other hand, if critical dissection only cuts off contact from Inner levels of spiritual supply, then the whole purpose of the phrase is defeated, and it becomes meaningless for that moment at least.

Sometimes it is surprising how purely intellectual interventions will arise unexpectedly as each point is approached while the Rite is being worked. The thing to do is treat these as notes to be dealt with afterwards, and dismiss them into mental storage for that purpose. They will keep there, and be all the better for a brief respite. A great deal of interesting information can be gathered in this way which adds to the importance of the Rite as a stimulator of imagination, if not a lot to its spiritual substance. For instance, as the phrase, "Leave of Life to live" is spoken, there could be a sudden idea spring up that perhaps the word "leave" ties somehow with "lief", meaning with will. Does this make the whole phrase mean "will to live"? An interesting speculation, but definitely something to deal with presently. Maybe a point to discuss in the Circle, but not one to occupy a mind during the Ritual action.

To get full value out of this Ritual, it has to be lived and experienced rather than academically analysed. Here, mind must be made to serve spirit. Man lives far better by love than by logic. This is a Rite to be savoured appreciatively like the Feast of Faith it really is. Each course has its own flavour, and in order to get the full taste it is necessary to have an appropriate appetite. It is truly said that hunger makes the best sauce, and if this Ritual is to be spiritually satisfying, then there should be a sort of hunger by the human souls participating in it for the Inner sustenance it has to offer. This ought not to be difficult nowadays, when so many people are satiated with material supplies, yet starving to death spiritually. What between spiritual starvation in some areas and physical malnutrition in others, we live in a very needy world. With this Ritual an attempt is made at balancing both types of hunger, for it combines a symbolic "Sacred Meal" with a good old-fashioned gorge afterwards. Those intending to make the most of these would be well advised to come fasting to the Feast and partake of the "Faith-food" first.

In times gone by, the best way of getting maximum effect from this type of Rite was to start by arriving in a suitable state of stress. Tired enough to feel triumphant at reaching the site safely, but not so exhausted as to be near collapse. Hungry enough to have a keen and appreciative appetite in the mood to eat almost anything, yet not so ravenous that thoughts of food exclude all other ideas. In other words, a balance-edge between extremities of endurance. A midpoint of dynamism, reached by drives from Inwardly applied discipline. That is certainly a very reliable method for reaching precisely the right degree of readiness to participate in the Ritual most profitably. Moderns who come comfortably in cars already full of food and well wined deserve all the disappointment they are sure to have. Not a single spiritual sensation are they likely to feel. There is no substitute for a correctly conditioned state of psycho-consciousness caused by skilfully applied stress in exactly the proper proportions.

The principle of this is illustrated by the old example of a bowstring. If strung too taut the bow would snap, and if too limply it would not operate at all. Similarly with humans. If too tense they will break, and if too slack they will not react. To ensure the most flexible and practical degree of response, the tension has to be at precisely the proper pitch needed. If people were musical instruments (which they are in a way), this would be a matter of tuning them up to their natural frequency. Before a bow can be fired or an instrument played, the strings have to be pressurised perfectly. So likewise must it be with those who hope for results by rituals. They, too, have to be properly tuned before their aim may be accomplished.

So, to practise this Ritual in an unprepared or unfavourable frame of mind and spiritual approach would be rather a waste of time and effort, apart from whatever entertainment might be obtained from the exercise. Unless a really deepdown need of the Rite is felt almost like a physical necessity for food, shelter, and warmth, it is probably best not to attend an occasion of it. That was, and still is, the only fundamentally valid motive which will ever make Rituals of this nature mean anything much for Mankind. Sheer spiritual necessity which calls for satisfaction over and above all other bodily or mental demands. In point of fact, this Rite offers fulfilment for all three, but the last two can so easily be obtained elsewhere nowadays.

That such a sort of necessity exists all over this Earth as much in our times as ever previously is only too evident. Strangely enough, there is nowhere so big a demand for Divinity as among atheists—if anyone alive may honestly be called so. Mostly, "atheism" means no more than a total rejection of other people's conceptions of a Consciousness extending throughout Cosmos. It is not so much a denial of Life, as a refusal to accept limits imposed on it by any other intelligence apart from the atheists themselves. This, of course, sets the very smallest limits to Life which they can possibly remain in and continue living. Did they but realise their opportunity, such is about the best position from which to start delving into themselves in search of their own Inner Identities, and it is quite incredible what this leads to. None become more convinced of an Infinite Intelligence behind the whole of Cosmos than those who find the very least trace of this in themselves or their lives. There is nothing, in the esoteric meaning of the term, like a Deity who has to be discovered by the individual efforts of anyone acting on their own initiative. That is exactly what "Initiation" signifies.

There comes a time in the lives of all mankind when their toys have to be exchanged for tools if ever they are to stand on their own feet and earn their livings in this, or any, world. We are reaching that collective stage in our human history about now. Through the past we made up some very pretty toys and all sorts of games to occupy ourselves with. It was a pity in a way that the first big blast we sounded on our scientifically designed horn blew so many of them to pieces. Still, sooner or later, they had to go. No need to cry for them, because their replacements will enable us to make even closer and better relations with the Living Spirit of Cosmos than ever before. Why regret the passing of uncertain faith-formularies associated with churches or temples when the oldest and longest Life-Faith always awaits those who care enough to seek it in their own Circles? The Spirit of Life does not alter in or as Itself. We just keep going round and round Its nucleus of Infinite energy transforming our share of this into whatever we will.

We have traced our Life-pattern back to the Stone Circles, and followed it forward to its cyclotron stage. Now we have to go on again with the same pattern until we catch up with its past projections into the future as cycles of pure Living Energy creating Cosmos out of consciousness. There is nothing truly new in this. Once the circuit design of Cosmic Life is set up, we can only keep following its paths or become burnt up if we impede its energies more than our limits of tolerance will endure. If, by some means, we were able to lay out a simile of such a circuit in ourselves and then live along those lines, we should certainly become able to adapt with whatever changes in Life our Cosmos is capable of. That is the object of this particular Ritual. To arrange the course of our consciousness in keeping with Cosmos by setting out a symbolic synthesis of its structure, so that if we follow it conscientiously enough we shall ultimately come to terms of truth with the Laws of Life.

The Stones have done more than stand for men meeting in an Earthly circle, or indicate individual positions of particular people. Their Cosmic counterparts have marked the place of all Mankind in the whole of Creation. They show our standing in relation to the remainder of our Life-companions everywhere. The sign of a Standing Stone represents our human heredity on this planet and points toward the stars which we shall have to reach and resurrect ourselves among if Man is to continue living after Doomsday here. Symbolically, a Standing Stone is sacred to the memory of everyone who ever lived on Earth and a salutation to forthcoming generations everlastingly. Once, a flat Earthstone and a standing Sky Stone together meant the Power of Parenthood, or Life on a Divine scale. Very much later, these were turned into a long shafted cross erected on its base. Still sacred. They always will be in one form or another.

Somehow, we ought to get away from ideas that a Standing Stone is only an outworn sign of our past, and see it as an upraised Finger of Fate beckoning us ahead toward our future. The Stone is not merely a memorial of bygone beliefs, but a pointer that should raise our highest hopes of finding faith in all the Life that lies ahead of us. With its sublime symbology of rising from Earth toward Heaven, it tells the entire story of humanity at a simple stroke. That is the whole point of our being here at all. If only we could get this into our heads until it reached our hearts deeply enough, we should hear the silent, secret speech of the Stones in our souls. Maybe it needs a good Stone to hammer this point home.

Those who missed that point in early days were the ancestors of others who tried to pick it up again centuries afterwards in the shape of the Philosopher's Stone which symbolised "Wealth without Work", or perhaps "Power over People". Anyone holding the secret of unlimited gold could buy up the whole world and everybody in it. What if that secret has not only been discovered, but is being ambitiously applied at the present time? Not with physical gold, of course, but by the greed for gain it seems to signify on lowest levels. Suppose the old Circle system has been converted into a Computer system in which all humanity is being set up for the purpose of coming under one control point? This is in no sense of being a science-fiction nightmare, but a cold and calculating certainty if no spiritual safeguards are strongly enough realised.

There is no doubt that "computerisation of civilisation" not only can, but is actually being done. Precisely for whose profit is beside the point here, but obviously whoever presses the top buttons has the biggest handouts. What matters is the principle involved. The Sacred Circle should be one of Companionship, and never one of compulsion or coercion. Every Stone had to speak for itself once, and still should. They stood together because they prayed, played, and paid together. They *came* into Circles of their own wills in the times when Sacred Circles stood for what mattered most in Mankind, Individualism coming into companionship with Cosmos. Then they began to break as Man broke faith with Life and forgot what we were supposed to stand for. Now, our chance has come again to re-combine ourselves not into new Circles, but the oldest of all, formed by perimeters of people round their common Faith in Life and confidence in one another. Humanity has now to show what it has come to after all this time away from its ancestral Stone Circles. Does it indeed have enough individualistic development of its original ideals to direct its own destiny toward ultimate Divinity? Or has it become no more than a helpless and rather hopeless herd ready to be rounded up into whatever corrals its purchasers please? Are both these extremities applicable to present Earth life? and is there another alternative available? In what Circles can we come to such conclusions and work out our best ways of coping with them?

To ask questions of Life and then live long enough to learn the answer is one main reason why the Rollright Ritual is phrased in its particular formulae. Providing we do not expect an instant answer, we have every right to ask of Life what we will. We are receiving in our present period of history replies to queries raised like Stones a very long while ago among us. If the questions had never been raised in the first place, they would not have been answered now. Not all of them are cleared away yet by any means, but that need not prevent us from asking others which propose problems at present. The only way for Man to learn anything of Life is to ask the Universal Awareness thereof a specific and straightforward question, then go on working until human consciousness becomes capable of translating the answer into terms we can understand. The answer to our Life-questions are there all the time, contained by Infinite Cosmic Intelligence. What we have to do is evolve our own capacity for comprehending them, and this is only possible at our best rate of Inner growth as individuals.

Once upon a time, intelligent investigators of Inner Life, or Initiates as they were later termed, sought until they found a suitable seeming Stone, then asked a question quietly into a hole it bore, afterwards giving their "self-signal" on its side with a series of knocks. They had sought, asked, and knocked in that order. They knew quite well that a physical Stone would not reply directly, but they also realised that the symbolic sense of the action connected their consciousness with an Inner Intelligence structured, so to speak, along such lines. No old time Initiate would have dreamed of expecting an instantaneous audible answer from a speechless Stone. Yet occasionally as opportunity occurred, he might have laid an actual ear against that same Stone and listened inside himself to learn if any reply had been received. What is more, he could have found some information awaiting him in this curious correspondence column written by who knew what "Holy Hand". Whether the Stone acted as a Key-Symbol opening his own connection with an Overmind, or impressions might be indeed gathered from the Stone itself by someone sensitive enough to detect and interpret them, scarcely matters if an advance of Life awareness becomes possible thereby. Man must use whatever means he may to make himself mean anything that matters as a Microcosm.

There is the greatest need nowadays among sincere and honest members of the human race to regain that strength of spiritual security which once prevailed among Stone Circlers, and should now be magnified a good deal more effectively by modern methods of Mankind. In the end, we have to overtake our beginnings again, and everywhere our Stones are waiting with "Welcome" written all over them in script which only spiritual sight may read. Then let us re-enter them not only with recognitive remembrance, but also with rejoicing at reunion with our oldest and our firmest friends on Earth. What else would wait so long and patiently for wandering families throughout the world to come once more together round the hearthstones of a hopeful Cosmic childhood.

Shall we be happy if we meet in this symbolic sort of Heaven? The old, old question born of infant innocence. A philosopher would say that happiness was relative, depending on so many factors. Any true Child of Cosmos could tell him otherwise. Happiness is loving Life as Love is lived. A Circle holding nothing, because nothing more is needed, therefore all is automatically included. Those are the sort of Circles we have to reconstruct again, building them this time from their equivalents in spiritual Stone.

Surely it is significant that Man's first action on the Moon was lifting up a piece of Stone? Have we now another chance of Life elsewhere than Earth, and will we really be much better than we were before? Infinite Intelligence alone could answer that, and, if It is also merciful, It will not tell us, but allow us all to find out for ourselves. From what finer platforms should we launch ourselves in search of spiritual Lifestates, than the faithful ones provided by those Circles which have stood for us so steadfastly in Stone? Who now knows or cares enough to claim Companionship therein and call with complete confidence:

HAIL HOLY LIVING SPIRIT! HERE COME I!

DERIVATION OF WORD "WITCH"

This unlucky word is one of the most misused and misleading terms in our modern vocabulary. The misinterpretation of "Witchcraft" as "The Craft of the Wise" seems traceable to Leland, an American folklorist of the 19th century. In his "Gypsy Sorcery" he says: "*Wicca* is a corruption of *witga* commonly used as a short form of *witega*, a prophet, seer, magician, or sorcerer." He goes on: "Wit and wisdom are near allied to witchcraft, and thin partitions do the bounds divide."

In fact, Leland had jumped to conclusions far too hastily. *Witega* is defined by the Anglo-Saxon Dictionary as : "A wise man, one who has knowledge, or knowledge from a superhuman source. A prophet." There was no suggestion whatever of alliance with *wicca*, which meant nothing but a witch in the worst sense. The Anglo-Saxon Dictionary defines witches and witchcraft as: "those who make love-philtres, poisons, put these in food or drink, or practise incantations." There is a specification in Latin of "malificus" (evildoer) and "venificus" (poisoner), also "prestigias" (trickster).

The Etymological Dictionary (Skeat, Oxford University Press) says: Wicked. Evil, bad, sinful. Originally a past participle with the sense "rendered evil" from verb *wikken*, obsolete adj. *wikke*—evil—once common usage. *Wikke* is allied to Anglo-Saxon *wicca* (masc) *wicce* (fem)—a witch. Allied to "weak", to give way. The feminine form is still used in the word "Witch".

In Greek, the word *witch* is equated with "pharmakis" or "drug-supplier" especially of poisonous and dangerous drugs.

Hebrew gives: AVB, an euphemism meaning "leather bottle" or "hollow belly", referring to ventriloquism, or producing fraudulent "spirit voices".

The oldest stem of the word appears to be from Teutonic-Iceland "vik", meaning weak, pliable, or easily bent. Thus a wicked person is one of weak character, easily bent or twisted out of shape. We still say; "bent on wickedness", or even a "bent" person.

There are many modern misbeliefs about the word. Some suppose a "wych-elm" (rowan tree) to be connected with witches. The term meant it had pliable or weak branches. Hence the description of wicker-work, or work with pliable stems. Again the suffix "wich" on place names has nothing to do with witches, it stems back to Latin "vicus" or place where people dwelt together.

Thus the entire contemporary confusion about the word "Witch" is due to expanded error and indifference to originally clear meanings. This has undoubtedly been encouraged by inadequate scholarship and irresponsible writers, especially in the case of sensational journalism.

Therefore the etymologically correct interpretation of a witch is a worker of wickedness in the sense of wrongdoing through the weakness of human nature. It should only be used in that form of meaning by anyone intending accuracy. Usage in other contexts is either mistaken, erroneous, or even libellous depending on circumstances. In earlier times the word was employed purely in derogatory terms as an insult or accusation of vicious behaviour. Sometimes survivors of primitive nature-faiths were accused of witchcraft by Christian authorities. They never used such a term to describe themselves, and there never has been a "Witch-cultus" of any kind in existence excepting a limited number of collectives formed for the specific purpose of practising evil among fellow-mortals. The description "White Witch" is quite inaccurate. By strict interpretations witches cannot be other than malicious and anti-social people.

CPSIA information can be obtained
at www.ICGtesting.com
Printed in the USA
LVOW11s1612250318
571082LV00002B/409/P

9 781908 011176